THE PATH

SUNDAY TIMES BESTSELLER

INTERNATIONAL BESTSELLER

'A worthy introduction to thinkers rarely taught in
British universities'

MATTHEW SYED, *THE TIMES*

—

'Smart . . . views our Western tradition through
an entirely different lens'

SUNDAY TIMES

—

'I couldn't wait for this. Brilliant. Fascinating'

JEREMY VINE, BBC RADIO 2

—

'Turns contemporary thinking around happiness on
its head . . . wonderfully simple and refreshing'

MARISA BATE, *THE POOL*

—

'A very accessible and inspiring piece of work . . . Anyone willing to
put the work in might find that this book really can change your life'

SENTINEL

—

'This is a book that turns the notion of help – and the self, for
that matter – on its head. Puett and Gross-Loh bring seemingly
esoteric concepts down to earth, where we can see them more
clearly. The result is a philosophy book grounded in the here and
now, and brimming with nuggets of insight'

ERIC WEINER

THE PATH

A New Way to Think
About Everything

**Michael Puett and
Christine Gross-Loh**

PENGUIN BOOKS

PENGUIN BOOKS

UK | USA | Canada | Ireland | Australia
India | New Zealand | South Africa

Penguin Books is part of the Penguin Random House group of companies
whose addresses can be found at global.penguinrandomhouse.com.

First published in the United States of America by Simon and Schuster 2016
First published in Great Britain by Viking 2016
Published in Penguin Books 2017

005

Printed in Great Britain by Clays Ltd, St Ives plc

A CIP catalogue record for this book is available from the British Library

ISBN: 978–0–241–97042–3

www.greenpenguin.co.uk

MIX
Paper from
responsible sources
FSC® C018179

Penguin Random House is committed to a
sustainable future for our business, our readers
and our planet. This book is made from Forest
Stewardship Council® certified paper.

It is not that the Way broadens humans; it is that humans broaden the Way.

—Confucius, the *Analects*

Contents

Foreword

Christine Gross-Loh

On a crisp, sunny morning in the fall of 2013, I sat in on a course at Harvard University on Chinese philosophy. I was there to write an article for the *Atlantic* on why an undergraduate class on such an arcane subject had become the third most popular on campus, after the predictable choices of introductory economics and computer science.

Professor Michael Puett, a tall, energetic man in his late forties, stood on the stage at Sanders Theatre speaking animatedly to over seven hundred students. His famously engaging lectures are done without any notes or slides—fifty minutes of pure talk every time. Students aren't assigned any readings except the translated words of the philosophers themselves: Confucius's *Analects*, the *Dao de jing,* the writings of Mencius. They are not assumed to have any prior knowledge of or interest in Chinese history or philosophy; they merely need to be open and willing to engage with these ancient texts. The course is well known for the bold promise the professor makes every year on the first day of class: "If you take the ideas in these texts seriously, they will change your life."

I'd completed a PhD in East Asian history at Harvard and, when I was a graduate student, taught undergraduates about Chinese philosophy. This material was not new to me. But as I listened to Michael that day and during the weeks that followed, I saw him bring these ideas to life in a way that I had never experienced before. He asked his students to not only grapple with the ideas of the thinkers but also to allow the ideas to challenge some of their fundamental assumptions about themselves and the world they are living in.

Michael speaks on Chinese philosophy at other universities and organizations throughout the world. After each talk, people invariably come up to him, eager to know how these ideas can apply to their own lives and real issues: their relationships, their careers, their family struggles. They realize that these principles present a fresh perspective on what it means to live a good and meaningful life; a perspective that stands at odds with so much of what they have assumed to be true.

It is a perspective that has affected many for the better. Michael's students have shared with me stories of how their lives were transformed by these ideas. Some have told me that they have changed the way they look at their relationships, now recognizing that the smallest actions have a ripple effect on themselves and everyone around them. As one student explained, "Professor Puett opened the door to a different way of interacting with the world around me, of processing my feelings, of establishing with myself, and with others, a sense of calm that I hadn't felt before."

These successful young people, positioned to become future leaders in whatever career they might pursue, told me how these ideas changed their approach to major life decisions and their own trajectory. Whether they decided to go into finance or anthropology, law or medicine, these ideas equipped them with different tools and a different worldview than those with which they had been raised, opening a new window onto the purpose of life and its infinite possibilities. One student told me, "It's very easy to have the mind-set that you're building toward some ultimate goal and climbing a ladder to some dream end—whether that's a certain position or a certain place in life. But this message really is powerful: that by living your life differently, you can open yourself up to possibilities you never imagined were even possible."

And it isn't just the philosophical texts that shape these students. Michael himself is an inspiration. He is known for his kindness, humility, and dedication to helping his students flourish: traits that come directly out of his decades of immersion in Chinese thought. "He completely embodies these teachings," one student said.

What is it about these philosophies that has such an impact on those who study them? None of these ideas is about "embracing yourself," "finding yourself," or following a set of instructions to reach a clear goal. In fact, they are the very antithesis of that sort of thinking. They are not specific, prescriptive, or grand. Rather, they are about changing from the ground up in unpredictable, unimaginable ways. One student explained how liberating it was to recognize that what we think is ingrained and inherent really isn't so: "You can adopt new habits and literally change the way you take in the world, react to it, and interact with other people. I learned that you can wield that power of habit, or 'ritual,' to achieve things that you never thought were possible, given who you thought you are."

We have long looked at Chinese thought through the wrong lens, tending to see it as inextricable from a "traditional" world and therefore considering it irrelevant to our contemporary lives. But as these students can attest, the teachings of the ancient Chinese philosophers force us to question many of the beliefs we take for granted. Their ideas on how people approach the world—how they relate to others, make decisions, deal with life's ups and downs, attempt to influence others, choose to conduct their lives—are just as relevant today as they were two thousand years ago. In fact, they are more relevant than ever.

Michael and I realized that these ideas can speak to all of us, and that's how this book came into being. On the pages that follow, we will show how the teachings of these Chinese philosophers can offer possibilities for thinking afresh about ourselves and about our future.

THE PATH

Preface

Confucius. Mencius. Laozi. Zhuangzi. Xunzi. Some of these thinkers might be familiar to you; others you have probably never heard of. One was a bureaucrat-turned-teacher who spent his life instructing a small coterie of disciples. Another roamed from region to region providing guidance to local rulers. Yet another was later thought to have been a god. Their lives and their writings seem obscure to us now, far removed from our modern lives.

After all, what could Chinese philosophers who lived over two thousand years ago possibly have to teach us about the art of living? You probably think of them, if you think of them at all, as placid wise men who spouted benign platitudes about harmony and nature. Today, meanwhile, we lead dynamic, liberated, modern lives. Our values, mores, technology, and cultural assumptions are completely different from theirs.

What if we told you that each of these thinkers offers a profoundly counterintuitive perspective on how to become a better human being and how to create a better world? What if we told you that if you take them seriously, the ideas found in these extraordinary texts from classical China have the potential to transform how you live? That is the central theme of this book: that the teachings of these ancient Chinese philosophers, who were responding to problems very much like our own, offer radical new perspectives on how to live a good life.

Most of us think we're doing the right thing when we look within, find ourselves, and determine what our lives should become. We figure out what kind of career would fit best with our personality and proclivities. We think about what sort of person would make a good match for us. And we think that if we find these things—our true self, the career we were meant to have, and our soul mate—life will be fulfilling. We will be nurturing our true self and living out a plan for happiness, prosperity, and personal satisfaction.

Whether we realize it or not, this vision of how to build a good life is rooted in history, specifically sixteenth-century Calvinist ideas about predestination, a chosen "elect," and a God who has laid out a plan for each individual to fulfill. The Calvinists rejected the following of ritual, which they saw as empty and formulaic, and instead emphasized sincere belief in this higher deity. Today we no longer think in terms of predestination, a chosen elect, or even, for some of us, God. But much of our current thinking is a legacy of these early Protestant views.

Many of us now believe that each of us should be a unique individual who knows himself. We believe we should be authentic, loyal to a truth we now tend to locate not in a higher deity but within ourselves. We aim to live up to the self we were meant to be.

But what if these ideas that we believe enhance our lives are actually limiting us?

We often associate philosophy with abstract, even unusable, ideas. But the strength of the thinkers in this book lies in the fact that they often illustrated their teachings through concrete, ordinary aspects of daily life. They believed that it's at that everyday level that larger change happens, and a fulfilling life begins.

As we explore these thinkers, our hope is that you will allow them to challenge some of your most cherished notions. Some of their ideas may make intuitive sense; others won't. We don't necessarily expect that you will agree with everything you read. But the very encounter with ideas so different from our own allows us to recognize that our assumptions about a good way to live are just one set among many. And once you recognize that, you can't return to your old life unchanged.

1

The Age of Complacency

A certain vision of history has become conventional wisdom. Until the nineteenth century, human beings lived in what we call "traditional societies." In these societies, they were always told what to do. They were born into a preexisting social structure that determined their lives: born peasants, they remained peasants; born aristocrats, they remained aristocrats. The family into which they were born determined how much money and power they had, and so the trajectories of their lives were set from the day of their birth.

The story continues: in nineteenth-century Europe, people finally broke free of these constraints. For the first time, we realized that we are all individuals who can think rationally. We can make decisions for ourselves and take control of our lives. As rational creatures, we can create a world of unprecedented opportunity. With these realizations, the story says, the modern world was born.

But if some of us broke away, other cultures were left behind—or so we believe. To many of us, classical China represents the ultimate traditional society in which people were required to follow rigidly defined social roles in order to live within a stratified, ordered world.

Thus, it must be a world that has nothing to teach us.

Of course, at times this reading of traditional societies in general and China in particular has been given a romanticized spin: *We now are alienated from each other, but people in the traditional world saw themselves as living in harmony with the cosmos. We have broken from the natural world and seek to control and dominate it, but people in the traditional world tried to live in accordance with the patterns of nature.*

This sentimental view of a traditional world, too, has nothing to teach us. It simply turns these so-called traditional societies into something akin to nostalgia pieces. We can go to a museum and see an Egyptian mummy and think, *How interesting.* An ancient Chinese artifact? *How quaint.* Intriguing to look at, but we wouldn't want to go back to that time—to the world they represent. We wouldn't want to live there or take any lessons from these traditional worlds, because they weren't modern. *We* are the ones who finally figured out things, not them.

But as you are about to learn, many of our stereotypes about these "traditional" societies are wrong. And there is much we can learn from the past.

The danger of our vision of history isn't just that it has led us to dismiss much of human existence as irrelevant, but also that we think today's predominant ideas are the only ones that encourage people to determine their own lives; therefore, today's ideas are the only correct ones.

The fact is that there has been a wide range of visions of how humans can lead lives of their own making. Once we recognize that, we can see the "modern" for what it actually is: one narrative out of many, built from a specific time and place. An entire world of thought thus becomes available to us—one that challenges some of our most cherished myths.

Myth: We Live in an Age of Freedom Unlike Any Other

Most of us think of ourselves as essentially free, in ways that our ancestors were not. After we in the West broke from the traditional world in the nineteenth century, we finally had the ability to decide for ourselves how to organize the world. We spent two centuries grappling with various competing ideologies: socialism, fascism, communism, and democratic capitalism. And once all but one of those ideas was largely discredited, we finally arrived at the "end of history." With the fall of the Berlin Wall in 1989, neoliberalism seemed to have won out as the one correct way of organizing the world—the one that best enables humans to flourish and prosper.

But what do we make, then, of the unhappiness, narcissism, and anxiety surging in the developed world? We are told that hard work will lead to success, yet the gap between rich and poor has widened dramatically, and social mobility is on the decline. Our lives are mediated by all kinds of fascinating and impressive devices, we have achieved unprecedented medical advances, yet we face environmental and humanitarian crises on a frightening scale. Several decades later, our great optimism has disappeared. We no longer feel as confident as we did in the way we have structured our world.

So how much *have* we figured out? Will historians look back on this era as one of prosperity, equality, freedom, and happiness? Or will they instead define the early twenty-first century as an age of complacency: a time when people were unhappy and unfulfilled; when they witnessed growing crises but failed to respond, feeling there to be no viable alternatives?

The Chinese philosophical texts described in this book offer alternatives to this Age of Complacency. But they are not coherent ideologies that would, for example, replace democracy. Rather, they are counterintuitive notions about the self and its place in the world. And many of them were actually developed in opposition to the idea of living according to any overarching system of thought.

From roughly 600 to 200 BC, an explosion of philosophical and religious movements throughout Eurasia gave rise to a wide variety of visions for human flourishing. During this period, which has come to be called the Axial Age, many of the ideas that developed in Greece also emerged in China and vice versa. In fact, in China, as we will see, certain beliefs arose that were very similar to those common in the West today. But in China, such views lost the day, while other ideas emerged in opposition, arguing for a very different path to a good life.

None of what we are looking at should be considered "Chinese" views as opposed to "Western" ones, any more than we are dealing with traditional ideas as opposed to modern ones. As we explore these concepts, we will see that not only have people been debating how best to organize the world since long before the modern era but also that there are true alternatives in thinking about how to live well.

Myth: We Know How to Determine the Direction Our Lives Will Take

When it comes to planning for happiness and prosperity in the West, we are taught to rely on our rational minds, confident that we can arrive at a solution by careful calculation. In the face of life's uncertainty, we take comfort in the belief that by overcoming emotion and bias and reducing our experience to measurable data, we can master chance and defy fate. Consider our most popular approach to moral and ethical dilemmas: inventing a representative hypothetical situation and working through it rationally. In the famous trolley experiment, we're told to imagine ourselves in a trolley yard, watching a runaway trolley coming down the tracks. We see it's going to hit five people up on the tracks ahead. But if we pull a switch we can divert the trolley onto a different track, where one person is lying. Do we allow the trolley to plow into those five people, or do we pull the switch to save them— actively choosing to kill the single person lying there?

What's the right thing to do?

This kind of question has occupied philosophers and ethicists for lifetimes. Countless essays—even a book or two—have been written on its implications. The scenario allows us to reduce decision making to a simple set of data and a single choice. Most of us think that's how decisions get made.

They tried these thought experiments in classical China, too. But our Chinese thinkers weren't as intrigued. This is a fine intellectual game, they determined, but you can play these games all day long, and they will have no impact on how you live your ordinary everyday life. None whatsoever.

The way we think we're living our lives isn't the way we live them. The way we think we make decisions isn't how we make them. Even if you did find yourself in that trolley yard someday, about to see someone killed by an oncoming trolley, your response would have nothing to do with rational calculation. Our emotions and instincts take over in these situations, and they guide our less spontaneous decisions as well, even when we think we're being very deliberate and rational: What should I have for dinner? Where should I live? Whom should I marry?

Seeing the limitations of this approach, these Chinese philosophers went in search of alternatives. The answer, for them, lay in honing our instincts, training our emotions, and engaging in a constant process of self-cultivation so that eventually—at moments both crucial and mundane—we would react in the right, ethical way to each particular situation. Through those responses, we elicit positive responses in those around us. These thinkers taught that in this way, every encounter and experience offers a chance to actively create a new and better world.

Myth: The Truth of Who We Are Lies Within Us

The breakdown of old aristocratic religious institutions left the people of the Axial Age in search of new sources of truth and meaning. Similarly, in our own age, we feel we have broken free of older, confining ways of thinking and are looking for new sources of meaning. Increasingly, we have been told to seek that higher truth within. The goal of a self-actualized person is now to find himself and to live his life "authentically," according to an inner truth.

The danger of this lies in believing that we will all know our "truth" when we see it, and then limiting our lives according to that truth. With all this investment in our self-definition, we risk building our future on a very narrow sense of who we are—what we see as our strengths and weaknesses, our likes and dislikes. Many Chinese thinkers might say that in doing this, we are looking at such a small part of who we are potentially. We're taking a limited number of our emotional dispositions during a certain time and place and allowing those to define us forever. By thinking of human nature as monolithic, we instantly limit our potential.

But many of the Chinese thinkers would argue that you are not and should not think of yourself as a single, unified being. Let's say that you think of yourself as someone with a temper; someone who gets angry easily. The thinkers we are about to encounter would argue that you should not say, "Well, that's just the way I am," and embrace yourself for who you are. As we will see, perhaps you aren't inherently an angry person. Perhaps you simply slipped into ruts—patterns of behavior—that you allowed to define who you thought you were. The truth is that you have just as much potential to be, say, gentle or forgiving as you do to be angry.

These philosophers would urge us to recognize that we are all complex and changing constantly. Every person has many different and often contradictory emotional dispositions, desires, and ways of responding to the world. Our emotional dispositions develop by looking *outward*, not inward. They are not cultivated when you retreat from the world to meditate or go on a vacation. They are formed, in practice, through the things you do in your everyday life: the ways you interact with others and the activities you pursue. In other words, we aren't just who we are: we can actively make ourselves into better people all the time.

Of course, this is no simple task. It requires us to change our mind-set about our own agency and about how real change happens. Nor is it a quick process:

change comes incrementally, through perseverence. It comes from training ourselves to broaden our perspective so that we can grasp the complicated tangle of factors (the relationships we're in, the company we keep, the jobs we hold, and other life circumstances) that shape any given situation and slowly transform our interactions with everything around us. This broad perspective enables us to behave in ways that gradually bring about true change.

While we have been told that true freedom comes from discovering who we are at our core, that "discovery" is precisely what has trapped so many of us in the Age of Complacency. We are the ones standing in our own way.

* * *

Does this mean that we need, then, a radical new plan for how to live and how to organize the world? On the contrary, the philosophers we will explore often illustrated their ideas through mundane aspects of daily life, arguing that this is where great change occurs. Following their lead, we have included many quotidian examples in this book to bring their ideas to life. But these thinkers did not mean for these illustrations to be taken as prescriptive advice, and nor do we. Rather, they are meant to show that we already do many of these things; we just don't do them well. As we rethink these aspects of our lives, we will understand how practical and doable the ideas really are.

The title of this book comes from a concept the Chinese philosophers referred to often as the *Dao*, or the Way. The Way is not a harmonious "ideal" we must struggle to follow. Rather, the Way is the path that we forge continually through our choices, actions, and relationships. We create the Way anew every moment of our lives.

There was no one unified vision of the Way with which all these philosophers would have agreed. Not only did they argue against the conventions of their own society, but also each offered a strikingly different vision of how exactly one creates this path. But they agreed that the very process of building it has endless potential to transform us and the world in which we live.

2

The Age of Philosophy

Enter any major museum of art, and you face a wealth of galleries: Mesopotamia. Ancient Egypt. Ancient Greece. Roman Empire. Medieval Europe. Modern Europe. Each gallery is filled with beautiful artifacts, and as you walk through them in succession, you can trace the rise of civilization. You can then wander to another wing if you like, and go into rooms focused on lands such as India, and China, and Japan.

This is how we tend to learn about world history: as discrete civilizations that developed on their own over time.

Now imagine a different kind of museum, one organized solely by era. You could stroll through a gallery, for example, and see a Roman silver denarius coin, a bronze coin from China's Han dynasty, and a punch-marked coin from India's Mauryan Empire. You would see right away that three major civilizations were going through remarkably similar changes at roughly the same time, despite the vast distance between them: each had become an empire, and each was running an economy based upon coin currency. Or you could enter a gallery about the early medieval period, several centuries later, and see Christian, Muslim, and Buddhist sacred objects and architectural remnants. They would vividly bring to life the fact that at the same time in history, all the major world religions spread, establishing themselves along the trade networks that linked China, India, and the Mediterranean region This would present a more accurate portrayal of how this history unfolded, for Europe and Asia have always been interconnected.

* * *

Many of us think that globalization is exclusively a modern phenomenon—that technology and air travel have ushered in a new era in which societies that were closed off from one another now finally can be connected. But if that's the case, then why were Confucius, Socrates, and the Buddha addressing similar philosophical questions at roughly the same time 2,500 years ago, despite living in completely different places, separated by such great distances, and speaking completely different languages? The fact is that innovations, technologies, and ideas have been moving across the globe for a very long time. Dynamic tension and movement within Eurasia have defined much of its history. Confucius, Socrates, and the Buddha were responding to very similar societal catalysts.

To understand why philosophical debate emerged at all and why these thinkers focused on such similar problems, we have to understand the teeming, vibrant culture in which they lived and their ideas developed.

Nineteenth-century Europeans were not the first to think they were breaking away from the past and creating a completely new age. Similar eruptions have happened repeatedly throughout human history. One of the most significant occurred across Eurasia midway through the first millennium BC.

In a revolutionary historical shift, the Bronze Age aristocratic societies that had dominated Eurasia for two thousand years, passing power and wealth down exclusively through hereditary bloodlines, began to crumble. As these states collapsed, new forms of political experimentation arose —from radical democracy in Greece to centralized bureaucracies and legal systems in China. These new forms of statecraft helped to foster the beginnings of social mobility. And in the midst of the immense social changes that these states engendered, the religious institutions that had been embedded in the earlier aristocratic cultures fell as well.

As a result, religious and philosophical movements flourished across Eurasia. In classical Greece, this was the era of Socrates, Plato, and Aristotle, as well the Pythagoreans and the Orphics. In India, it brought the emergence of Jainism and, most important, the arrival of the Buddha. And in China, this was the age of Confucius, Mencius, and the other philosophical and religious movements we will be encountering in this book. All were roughly contemporary. And all were pondering the questions that emerge when a societal order breaks down: *What is the best way to run a state? How do I build a proper world where everyone has a chance to flourish? How do I live my life?* All were wrestling with problems very much like our own.

The Axial Age lasted until the formation of massive empires across Eurasia in the last centuries BC. In response to these empires, a series of salvationist religions spread through Eurasia in the first centuries of the Common Era: Christianity, Manichaeism, Mahayana Buddhism, Daoism, and, later, Islam. And within a few centuries, in many parts of Eurasia and especially in Europe, this period of philosophical and religious experimentation would come to an end after the fall of the empires and a return to aristocratic rule.

The societal changes of the Axial Age led to remarkably similar developments across a wide geographical area. There's no evidence that Confucius and the Buddha and the Greek philosophers were even aware of one another, much less one another's ideas. And yet by around the year 500 BC, these major philosophical movements in disparate parts of Eurasia were unified by the belief that the world had to change.

Throughout much of the Bronze Age, most humans saw no possibility of being able to change the trajectory of their lives, but increased social mobility now planted the seeds of the idea that what is available to some people could and should be available to all, not just a few.

At the same time, people saw themselves as living in a period of massive cultural crisis. The times were marked by ceaseless warfare, especially in Greece, north India, and the North China Plain—the very areas where many of the major philosophical and religious movements emerged later. In these regions, there was a pervasive sense that humans had lost their way and had forsaken the rules of conduct that enabled them to live in simple civility. The Greek poet Hesiod captured the ethos of the time, lamenting that he was living in an era when relationships had crumbled: fathers and offspring disagreed with one another, children failed to care for their aging parents, siblings fought with one another, and people freely gave their "praise to violence."

It was in the midst of this cultural crisis that religious and philosophical movements began emerging. Many involved withdrawing from society and creating alternative communities based upon a full rejection of violence. Others emphasized transcending the fallen world here on earth altogether by imagining a higher world beyond.

The movements that developed in the North China Plain focused, too, on creating alternate worlds. But for them, the solution was not to withdraw from society or seek higher, transcendent realms, but to make changes in the very patterns of everyday life.

Specific developments led to this focus on the mundane. In the North China Plain, one response to the breakdown of the Bronze Age hereditary societies was the formation of new states run by literati from the class just below the aristocracy, who would hold their positions through merit rather than through birth. More and more people sought to become educated in the hope of gaining positions in these new bureaucracies and raising their status in life. As they became educated, they became deeply dissatisfied with the world as it was and began to ponder how to live differently. Most of the new religious and philosophical movements in China during this period were populated by figures from this growing literati class.

Take Confucius, for example. This great philosopher lived during the decline of the last great Bronze Age dynasty, the Zhou dynasty. The Zhou was a powerful aristocratic clan that claimed its status over other great clans because it possessed the mandate of Heaven. In early China, Heaven was seen as a deity that granted the most virtuous lineage of the time the mandate to rule for as long as it continued to be moral. It was an age very much like pre-nineteenth-century Europe, in which the great aristocratic lineages ruled through a claim of divine right.

During Confucius's lifetime, these leading aristocratic families were losing their power. The Zhou itself was in decline, but so were the other clans. None could step forward to claim the new mandate.

It was during the ensuing political vacuum that figures such as Confucius came to prominence. He held a few minor official posts and, later in his life, became a teacher who focused on a new generation of people seeking these positions as well.

When we think about Confucianism today, we often associate it with rigid social hierarchy, strict gender roles, and a conservative emphasis on correct behavior—an impression based in part on later reinterpretations of these teachings. But the portrayal of Confucius in the *Analects* is not one of someone who was trying to control people, nor is it one of someone who was trying to create a coherent ideology at all. On the contrary, we see a figure trying to create worlds in which humans could flourish. These worlds were to be built in the here and now, through how we interact with those around us.

Confucius thought that a great era of human flourishing had existed in the early days of the Zhou, about five hundred years before his lifetime. He saw this period as having been ruled by several individuals who cultivated themselves, became virtuous, and, briefly, succeeded in creating a better world around themselves. He sought to do the same: create a world where his students could thrive, with the hopes that some of them might be able to create a larger social order where the broader population could flourish too.

Every philosopher we encounter in this book is similar to Confucius. Each emerged from this crucible of transition. Each opposed the society in which he lived and was actively contemplating new and exciting ways to live. Each believed strongly that every person has equal potential for growth.

And these thinkers' training led them to be extremely practical and concrete. This is why, in questioning their society, they tended not to focus on big abstract questions immediately. Rather, they asked, How did our world become like this, and what can we do to change it? Out of these practical questions emerged inspiring discoveries about each person's potential to be great and good.

3

On Relationships: Confucius and As-If Rituals

I f we told you that playing a simple game of hide-and-seek with a four-year-old could dramatically transform all your relationships, we'd understand if you were skeptical. But the fact is that when you play this game—when you crouch with your foot sticking out of a closet door so that she can find you easily, when she laughs with glee upon discovering you, and when you enthusiastically repeat the game with her again and again—you are not just engaging in lighthearted play. The two of you are participating in a ritual by taking on roles that diverge from your usual ones—a ritual that allows you to construct a new reality.

This may seem counterintuitive. We tend to think of ritual as something that tells us what to do, not as something transformative. But one strand of classical thought, beginning with Confucius, led to a radically new vision of exactly what ritual can do.

Confucius, who lived from 551 to 479 BC, was the first great philosopher in the Chinese tradition. His vast and enduring influence comes not from grand ideas but from deceptively simple ones—ideas that flip on its head everything we understand about getting to know ourselves and getting along with other people.

Consider this passage from Book 10 of the *Analects,* a collection of conversations and stories compiled by Confucius's disciples after his death:

"He would not sit until he had straightened his mat."

Here's another one:

"He would not teach while eating."

Not quite what you were expecting? Seems a little too prosaic for one of humanity's most important texts?

These passages are not exceptional. The *Analects* is full of concrete, minute details about what Confucius did and what he said. We find out how high Confucius holds his elbows. We see how he talks to different people when he walks into a room. We learn, in specific detail, how Confucius behaves at dinnertime.

You might wonder how any of this could be of philosophical significance. You might be tempted to flip through the book for yourself and search for passages where Confucius says something really profound. But to understand what makes the *Analects* a great philosophical work, we need to learn how Confucius comported himself at his meals. We need to know what he did on a daily basis. The reason these daily moments are important is because, as we will see, they are the means through which we can become different and better human beings.

Such a stance is rare in the field of philosophy. If you take most any philosophy class or read a philosophical work, chances are the philosopher will jump right in with big questions such as: *Do we have free will? What is the meaning of life? Is experience objective? What is morality?*

But Confucius took the opposite approach in his teachings. Rather than start with the great big philosophical questions, he asked this fundamental and deceptively profound question:

How are you living your life on a daily basis?

For Confucius, everything began with this question—a question about the tiniest things. And unlike the big, unwieldy questions, this is one we all can answer.

The Fragmented World

We often think of people from traditional cultures as having believed in some sort of harmonious cosmos that dictated how they ought to live and the social roles they would be confined to playing. This is certainly how many in the West have thought about China. But the truth is that many Chinese philosophers actually saw the world very differently: as consisting of an endless series of fragmented, messy encounters.

This worldview emerged from the notion that all aspects of human life are governed by emotions, including the endless human interactions that take place. The *Nature That Emerges from the Decree*, a recently discovered fourth-century BCE text, taught that

> *The energies of joy, anger, sorrow, and sadness are given by nature. When it comes to their being manifested on the outside, it is because they have been elicited by others.*

All living things have dispositions, or tendencies to respond to things in certain ways. Just as a flower has an inherent disposition to lean toward the sun, and birds and butterflies are disposed to seek out flowers, human beings have dispositions too. Our disposition is to respond emotionally to other people.

We often don't even notice how constantly our emotions are being drawn out from us. But our feelings sway back and forth, depending on what we encounter. We experience something pleasurable and then feel pleasure; we encounter something frightening and subsequently feel fear. A toxic relationship makes us feel despair, an argument with a coworker makes us livid, a rivalry with a friend arouses jealousy. We find ourselves experiencing certain emotions more often than we do others, and our responses then become patterned habits.

This is what life is about: moment after moment in which people encounter one another, react in an infinite number of ways, and are pulled to and fro emotionally. Not one of us can escape this, be it a child on a playground or the leader of a great nation. Every single human event is shaped by the world of our emotional experiences. If human life consists of people constantly bumping up against one another and reacting passively, we live in a fragmented world, one in which we are buffeted about endlessly by disparate events.

But all is not hopeless: we can refine the way we react during these endless encounters and create pockets of order. The *Nature That Emerges from the Decree* argues that we should strive to move from a state where we just randomly respond to things emotionally (*qing*) to a state where we are able to respond with propriety, or "better ways of responding" (*yi*):

> *Only through training do we become able to respond well . . . At the beginning [of our lives] one responds through emotions; at the end, one responds through propriety.*

Developing propriety does not mean overcoming or controlling the emotions. Feeling emotion is what makes us human. It simply means cultivating our emotions so that we internalize better ways of responding to others. These better ways become a part of us. When we have learned to refine our responses, we can start to respond to people in ways that we have cultivated, instead of through immediate emotional reaction. We do this refining through ritual.

Customs and Rituals

Most of us have certain "rituals." Whether it's a morning cup of coffee, family dinners, a couple's regular Friday date night, or a piggyback ride for the kids at bedtime, we consider these moments important because they give our lives continuity and meaning and bond us to our loved ones.

Confucius would agree that all of these moments are potential rituals. But in his teachings, he elaborated upon what we should consider rituals and why they are significant.

Consider a simple act that we all engage in multiple times a day:

You run into a friend.

"Hey, how's it going?"

"Great! How about you?"

This brief act connects you for a moment before you continue on.

Or your colleague introduces you to someone new: "Great to meet you." You shake his hand, and then you both make breezy chitchat about the weather, the surroundings, or some recent news event.

Or you run into a close friend at the grocery store. You stop your carts and give each other a warm hug. "How have you been? How are the kids?" You talk a little bit about your lives, have a short, animated conversation, and promise to make a date for coffee before you go your separate ways.

We use different greetings, ask different sorts of questions, and use different tones of voice when talking to different people. We usually do all of this unconsciously. We subtly adjust our behavior, our phrases, the very words we use, depending on whether we are talking to a close friend, an acquaintance, someone we just met, our mother, our father-in-law, our boss, our coach, or our child's piano teacher. We modify the way we speak according to who we're with because we have learned this is the socially appropriate thing to do. And because we are with different people and in different situations all day long, everything we do shifts constantly.

Of course, any philosopher would have noticed that we employ different types of greetings and use different tones of voice in different circumstances. But few would have thought this to be philosophically significant.

That is where Confucius is different. He begins by observing that if we are spending the vast majority of our waking hours doing these things, then philosophically, that is exactly where we need to begin. We need to ask ourselves why we engage in these actions. These small acts are customs—conventions that we are socialized into performing. But at least some of these could be made into rituals—a term that Confucius defines in a new and provocative way.

* * *

Human beings are creatures of habit. We become accustomed to doing these small things—standing to the side to let a stranger pass by, putting on a tie for a job interview—and we do them unconsciously.

Even when we're not conscious of what we're doing, there is some good effect. If we are feeling a bit down, taking a moment to say hi to another person can interrupt a cycle of negative emotion. If we are greeting someone we've had a conflict with, we can share another, more civil side of ourselves and momentarily break the pattern of disagreement. For those brief moments, we experience different relationships with those around us.

But when we go through life performing most social conventions by rote, they lose their power to become rituals that can profoundly change us. They don't do much to help us become better people.

In order to help ourselves change, we must become aware that breaking from our normal ways of being is what makes it possible to develop different sides of ourselves. Rituals—in the Confucian sense—are transformative because they allow us to become a different person for a moment. They create a short-lived alternate reality that returns us to our regular life slightly altered. For a brief moment, we are living in an "as-if" world.

The As-If World

In early China, people saw human beings as a mass of contradictory elements—conflicting emotions, turbulent energies, chaotic spirits—all of which they worked to refine during their lives. But at the moment of death, a person's most dangerous energies—all of his anger and resentment at passing away while his loved ones go on living—would be released and haunt the living. Thus, people believed that the world was filled with the spirits of the deceased, who looked jealously upon their survivors. Death would bring out the worst in the living as well: horrible sadness, confusion, inexplicable anger.

To combat all of these negative, uncontrolled energies, people developed ritual acts, the most important of which was ancestral worship. The purpose was to transform dangerous ghosts into benevolent ancestors. The meat of a beast, most often a pig, would be placed in bronze ritual vessels and cooked over an open fire in front of the family at a temple. The family would call down the ghosts to feed on the rich smoke that rose up from the meat. By feeding the ghosts these offerings, the living hoped to humanize them, bring them back into the family, and persuade them to inhabit the role of a benevolent ancestor hovering above.

After the ritual had ended, the ancestor eventually reverted to an angry, haunting ghost, and the rite would have to be repeated.

In the *Analects,* Confucius is asked about ancestor worship. He says that the ritual is absolutely necessary but that it makes no difference whether the spirits are participating or not: "We sacrifice to them," he said, "*as if* they are there." What matters is participating in the ritual fully: "If I do not participate in the sacrifice, it is as if I did not sacrifice."

But if the ghosts aren't even necessarily there, why do the ritual as if they are?

In life, the relationship between the deceased and the living had been imperfect and fraught, as real-life human relationships are. A father might have been stern, unloving, and temperamental; his offspring might have been hostile and rebellious. These unresolved tensions haunt the living all the more painfully when the father dies, and any possibility of a reconciliation has ended. If performed well, the ritual moves us from this troubled world of human relationships and creates a space—a ritual space—in which ideal relationships can be forged. Within this space, it is as if the haunting ghosts are proper, beneficent ancestors to the living. The living now behave as if they were proper descendants of the ancestors. The angers, jealousies, and resentments that had existed between the living and the dead are being transformed into a vastly better relationship.

For Confucius, the ritual was essential because of what it did for the people performing it. To ask whether these ritual acts actually affected the deceased or not missed the point entirely. Family members needed to make the sacrifices because acting *as if* the ancestors were there brought about change within themselves.

The ritual also changed the feelings of the living toward one another. A death always engenders changes in relationships among those left behind. A long-dormant childhood rivalry between two siblings flares up again; a wayward son suddenly becomes the nominal head of the household, stirring unrest among the others. Within the ritual, however, all play their new familial roles as if there were no discord.

The power of the ritual lay in how patently distinct it was from the real world. Consider one variation of the rite in which three generations exchanged roles. A grandson would personify his deceased grandfather, while his own father would personify him. Each living descendant was made to take on the perspective of the person with whom he often experienced the most tension in the world outside.

This was clearly an as-if world: there was no way the participants could possibly mistake the roles they were playing for roles they could ever assume in real life; a father is not being trained to be the son of his son. But through this rite, the living would not only develop a different relationship toward the deceased. Those left behind would also be brought together into new relationships.

Of course, the ritual always ends. Family members walk out of the ritual space, and the moment they do, they are in the messy world again. Over time the fragile peace falls apart once more. Siblings squabble, cousins rebel, the father and son are still at odds with each other.

This is why families returned to the ritual repeatedly. The fragile peace might crumble once they left the temple, but gradually, by doing the rituals again and again and re-creating these healthier connections, the improved relationships among the family members would begin to manifest more in daily life.

The ritual does not tell anyone how to behave in the real world. The perfectly ordered world inside the ritual could never replace the flawed world of real-life relationships. It works because each participant plays a role other than the one he inhabits normally. That "break" with reality is the key for allowing the participants to begin to work on their relationships. A father's pretending to be his son helps him to understand his child and become a better father and a better person.

Sacrificing beasts and placating spirits may seem distant from our twenty-first-century lives, but the value of the rituals remains. We too are haunted by ghosts: the irritating relative we never get along with; the grudge we can't seem to shake off; the past we can't forget.

We tend to fall into patterned, habitual responses. They may be social conventions and customs we follow unthinkingly, like our greetings or the way we hold a door open for someone. They may be routines that we don't even notice, such as the whine we slip into when we're talking to a sibling on the phone, or a tendency to become quiet when distressed instead of expressing our needs clearly. But we do these things all the time. Some patterns are good, and some are less so. If we were always "true" to ourselves and behaved accordingly, we would be stuck in old behaviors, never forgiving, and limiting our potential to transform.

But we already know how to break these patterns.

When we visit a friend's family, for example, as outsiders we notice their routines and small actions: their Sunday morning pancake breakfast, the way they hug one another to say good morning. These rituals stand out to us because they are new to us. When we observe or even participate in them, we do so with a consciousness that we don't bring to our own lives.

When we travel, breaking from our everyday routine can allow us to develop new sides of ourselves. And when we return, we feel the lingering effects of those changes.

Why, then, don't we do this all the time? Perhaps it is because deliberately constructing ritual moments in our "real" lives feels contrived.

But as-if moments can lead to tremendous movement.

Let's return to the hide-and-seek game with the four-year-old that opened this chapter. How does this nurture a relationship? The game is an as-if ritual. It allows a shift in roles: the child, normally so vulnerable, gets to play at being a powerful person who bested an adult by finding him. The adult gets to play at being a bumbling person so inept that he can't even find a good hiding place. Of course, the child knows that the adult knows that she can see him, but part of the ritual is that they are playing as if she were able to outsmart him.

This role reversal breaks their usual pattern. The child gets to experience a feeling of competence that she will remember even after the game is over. The adult, usually an infallible being (at least in the eyes of a child), has now played at being fallible and vulnerable. He isn't really becoming a befuddled adult, but the role reversal helps him to develop more complex, nuanced sides of himself that he, too, can take with him into other situations: vulnerability, connection, levity, and the ability not to cling to power too tightly.

The key for the players is to be conscious that they are pretending; that together they have entered an alternate reality in which they imagine different sides of themselves. If they can do this, then not only will experiences like playing hide-and-seek help cultivate a mutually more joyful and respectful relationship, but also these accumulated moments will influence the sort of person each becomes over time. These repeated rituals will develop aspects of each of them that eventually enhance other relationships in both of their lives.

As-If Rituals

Why do we say "please" and "thank you"?

Three centuries ago, European society and social relations were still defined entirely by hereditary hierarchy. If a peasant were speaking to a lord, he would use certain deferential terms, and if an aristocrat were speaking down to a peasant, he would employ completely different terms in turn.

As markets began to develop in the cities, people from different classes began to interact in new ways. Rituals developed in which buyers and sellers could act as if they were equal, though they were anything but. The "please" and "thank-you" exchange was a brief moment in which participants could experience a semblance of equality.

We perform this as-if ritual as well. Imagine that you are at the dinner table, and your child (or nephew or grandchild) demands, "Give me the salt." If that child is very young, you understand that he hasn't learned social niceties yet, so you might say, "Okay, but what do you say . . . ?" or "What's the magic word?" He might not answer right away, and then you press him again. "What do you say . . . ?" And then you go back and forth until the child says, "*Please* give me the salt." Then you hand him the salt and walk him through the thank-you.

Why do we do this even though the child makes it clear he thinks it's ridiculous to be forced to go through this charade? This is a chance for him to enter a ritual in which he will act as if he were asking something of an equal. You are not doing it to program him to act a certain way; you are training him to learn what it means to ask something of a fellow human being and what it means to express gratitude.

If he learns the exchange merely as a rote act, then he hasn't learned it well. Of course, at first, it *is* a rote act, one of many he is socialized to perform as he grows up. But as he does this over and over, he begins to see why. He also understands how to tweak things. He sees how people respond to his "pleases" and "thank yous" and learns when saying these words is good enough or when some other words or a change of tone or expression would work better.

In fact, children intuitively understand ritual better than most adults do. They recognize that its value lies in the fact that it is not real. Think of a group of kids during imaginary play. One pretends to be a policeman defending a store against the others, who have become a gang of robbers. They wave around their guns, hide behind cushions, and shoot one another, over and over. The children don't see this gunplay as violence the way an adult might. For them the gunplay is play—separate from the real world. They are fully aware that this is pretend, and they repeat it because it allows them to step outside their lives and hone different sides of themselves: they learn to manage fears and anxieties or play the role of rescuer and hero, all in a safe environment of their own making.

If our parents told us about Santa Claus when we were young, that too was an as-if ritual. Families participate in the reality that he will come down the chimney with a big bag of toys. During the weeks leading up to Christmas, children write letters and make lists and are motivated to be on their best behavior. On Christmas Eve, they set out a plate of cookies and a glass of milk near the Christmas tree. Adults and older children feel motivated to do what they can to keep this fiction going for little children and create an atmosphere of joy. It doesn't really matter whether Santa Claus is real or not. What matters is that their behavior changes for the better, and they are brought closer to one another.

Living as-if is something we all did as children, and then more or less abandoned once we grew up and believed that we needed to behave more authentically. But we adults do have some ritual spaces as well. Think of a therapist's office, where people go to talk about their troubles during a set period of time. Although many of us assume that this time is helpful because we are slowly uncovering who we really are, from a Confucian standpoint, the greater benefit comes from the fact that we have set up a de facto ritual space in which we take on as-if roles that we cannot play outside. Therapy helps break the patterns that dominate our lives and, through the interactions between therapist and patient, allows us to construct very different ways of relating to others.

But inevitably, we fall back into old patterns outside the therapist's office. So we go to therapy weekly, sometimes for years, and keep on practicing breaking those old patterns. Through repetition, we slowly develop new ways of interacting and eventually construct a different and far better self.

We value the notion of truth, but the fact is that people in intimate relationships construct new realities with white lies all the time: "You're the greatest." "There's nothing to worry about." "You are the best cook ever." One of the most common of these is the phrase "I love you." Couples who are in the habit of saying this probably do not feel fully loving every second of the day. They almost certainly have a bevy of complicated feelings toward their partner from time to time. But there is a greater good in nurturing the relationship through such rituals that let them break from reality and enter a space where it's as if they do love each other fully and at every moment. At the moment that they express their love in an as-if way, they *are* really doing it.

Think about Book 10 of the *Analects*, filled with anecdotes of Confucius's everyday habits. He wasn't just straightening his mat because he liked things to look neat. He understood that seemingly minor actions such as arranging the place where people would sit with him would create a different environment that could affect them profoundly. The modern-day equivalent of the mat ritual might be our dinnertime routines: when we set the table, perhaps laying out placemats and napkins, even lighting candles, we step out of our regular lives and create an alternate reality for ourselves and those with us. Even if the day has been stressful, if there's been a lot of conflict, there's no need for someone to declare, "Okay, it's time to stop fighting and relax now." The dinner table ritual simply creates a break that allows everyone to enter a different mode.

But these moments when we engage in rituals in a Confucian way are exceptions. Confined by our commitment to authenticity, we seldom allow ourselves to act as-if. It feels like pretending, like child's play. Yet Confucius might well point out how contradictory it is that we resist rituals because we think they tell us what we should do, yet we unwittingly follow so many social norms and conventions. When we are blind to the value of the possible rituals that pervade our lives, we end up performing them by rote. *We* are the ones who are becoming automatons.

Some recognize the danger of this. On a few college campuses, initiatives such as Ask Big Questions have facilitators teach students to position themselves, create an atmosphere of trust, and phrase their statements so that highly charged debates (such as how to foster peace in the Middle East) do not break down into shouting matches. Students are literally taught the rituals—crafted and artificial though they may seem—of conversation: how to pose questions, stop and listen, and speak in ways that open up a space for engagement and progression instead of defensiveness and rigidity. In this way they are given the means to create an as-if world where they can break from patterns they may have fallen into (such as blurting out strong, emotional opinions), act civilly, and relate better to one another.

What would happen if we took steps to move out of the rote stage in which so many of us are stuck? Like the child learning to say "please" and "thank you," like the college students learning how to adopt a different demeanor to open themselves up to challenging ideas, we would see the value of all these alternate realities, of experiencing the tension between the way things are and the pocket of order we have created. We'd be training ourselves to develop better ways of engaging with others over the course of our lives.

This may seem like a surprising way to think about ritual or change in general. After all, our model for ritual is based so often upon things like a baptism, a wedding, a graduation: ceremonies in which we move from being

one thing (sinful creature, single person, student) to another (believer, spouse, graduate). There is a before and
an after, and through the rite, we are transformed.

Confucius offers a very different vision of transformation, which focuses not on the grand, dramatic event but
on the small repeated moments. Like saying "I love you,"
these as-if moments create moments of connection
throughout the day that build up slowly, but no less dramatically, over time.

The Malleable Self

Before we can be transformed through as-if rituals, we
have to let go of the mentality of the "true self."

Be sincere. Be authentic. Be true to who you are. These
slogans of the modern age encourage us to look within.
We struggle to uncover who we are and then embrace
what we see.

The danger is that what we discover is only a snapshot
of who we are at a particular time and place. We read
self-help books, meditate, write in our journals, and then
diagnose and label ourselves: *I'm a free spirit. I'm a hot-
head. I'm a dreamer. I fear intimacy. I moved around too
much as a child, and now I'm skittish when meeting new
people. My history of destructive relationships is due to my
cold relationship with my father.* By embracing these patterns, we allow them to harden. Such labeling begins in
childhood: *this one is studious; that one is temperamental.*
These labels drive our behavior and our decisions, and

become a self-fulfilling prophecy. As a result, too many of us wake up one day feeling stuck inside a narrow definition of ourselves.

What we in the West define as the true self is actually patterns of continuous responses to people and the world; patterns that have built up over time. For example, you might think, *I'm just the kind of person who gets annoyed easily*. On the contrary, it's more likely that you have *become* the kind of person who does get irritated over minor things because of how you've interacted with people for years. But that's not because you are, in fact, such a person. By being loyal to a "true self," you ended up concretizing destructive emotional habits.

Remember the teachings of *Nature That Emerges from the Decree*: just as the world itself is fragmented, we are too. Instead of thinking of ourselves as single, unified selves who we are trying to discover through self-reflection, we could think of ourselves as complex arrays of emotions, dispositions, desires, and traits that often pull us in different and contradictory ways. When we do so, we become malleable. We avoid the danger of defining ourselves as frozen in a moment in time.

A Confucian approach would be to note your patterns and then work actively to shift them. Over time, breaking those patterns—say, suppressing your usual sigh when your father starts in on one of his political tirades (even though you *are* irritated); or making it a point to greet your wife at the door when she gets home from work (even though you'd rather stay glued to your computer)—will allow different sides of you to emerge. Over time, you internalize a more constructive way of acting in the world instead of being led by your undisciplined emotional reactions. Little by little you develop parts of yourself you never knew existed, and you start becoming a better person.

* * *

Breaking patterns helps us recognize that other people are malleable too. Perhaps you've been having a conflict with your mother. She disapproves of your life choices, and she's made hurtful comments that seem intended to make you feel guilty. It's gotten to the point where just thinking about talking with her makes you feel alienated, and now you avoid it altogether. You just know that you will have the same conversation over and over, and the thought fills you with hopelessness.

In most cases like this, the problem between the two of you is not that your personalities are incompatible or that your mother is prone to guilt-tripping you. It's that your communication has fallen into a pattern. You're stuck in your roles: she's the harping mother, you're the recalcitrant offspring. Neither of you feels good about this, but you can't see any way out.

The way out is to recognize that you have fallen into a rut, but you can change it. Remember that your mother is not static or unchanging. She is a complex, multifaceted person. Think through what you can do or say to elicit other sides of your mother, and then behave as if you are speaking to those sides of her. Just as she has a tendency to nag and pressure you, she also has a desire to nurture her child or, at the very least, *feel* that she is nurturing her child. How could you alter the things you say or the tone of your voice to appeal to her nurturing side? By doing so, you are helping her to inhabit another role: that of a caring mother who wants to be there for her child.

Your gut reaction might be to protest, "But that isn't being real. It isn't how I really feel." Why should you change your own behavior purely to elicit another side of your mother and be generous when you're feeling resentful? But this comes from the mistaken idea that we should answer to some "core" self. We are always changing. Will we act according to where we are stuck in the moment, or will we act in a way that opens up a constellation of possibilities?

There is no one true self to uncover—in ourselves or in others. The psychologist and philosopher William James (1842–1910) once wrote, "A man has as many social selves as there are individuals who recognize him"—a surprisingly Confucian sentiment. Each of us has myriad roles that often conflict, and there is no norm that can tell us how to navigate them. Only the practice of rituals can help us learn how to do that.

Our patterned behaviors and rote habits—not rituals— are what really dictate our lives and get in the way of our caring for other people. But through a life spent doing as-if rituals that break these patterns, we gain the ability to sense how to be good to those around us. This is what matters. This is *ren,* or a sensibility of goodness.

The Importance of Goodness

Confucius's disciples frequently asked him to define goodness. He would give each of them a different answer each time, depending on the situation. That's because Confucian goodness is not something you can define in the abstract. It's the ability to respond well to others; the development of a sensibility that enables you to behave in ways that are good for those around you and to draw out their own better sides.

Everything we do either expresses goodness or detracts from it. You have probably experienced how the atmosphere in the room changes suddenly when someone comes storming in. But you might not have noticed how a stranger's frown affected you when you were just walking down the street. That passing frown can subliminally influence your mood and lead to a cascade of reactions. Over the course of the day, you are not the only one who ends up changed by that minor passing frown. Other people you encounter do too because they are affected by you.

To understand how much we affect others, try tweaking some of your typical behaviors. See what happens when you glare at your best friend, say hello exuberantly to your company's taciturn CEO in the elevator, or put your backpack on the just-vacated seat next to you on the subway at rush hour. And then try acting differently: open a door for a stranger, text a friend who is having relationship problems, gently help your grandmother cross a patch of ice. Take note of how all these changes affect you and those with you.

Confucius would not define goodness; he wanted his disciples to know that we must feel it in all these different, shifting situations to understand what it means to express it. We have all felt it, and once we recognize it, we can develop it further.

Expressing Goodness

How do you help a friend who's going through a hard time?

For many ethicists, this would probably not be a significant question. They tend to focus on generic issues that we can rationally calculate in broader ways. They often choose examples, like the trolley experiment mentioned in our introduction, that are abstracted completely from the complexities of everyday life—thought experiments in which the only goal is to solve a clearly defined problem through rational deliberation. In its purest form, the trolley experiment leaves no room for ambiguities such as how your decision would change if one of the five people were your mother, say, or if all five were children. These ethicists would say that if you let such factors affect your decision, in fact, you are not being rational; you are allowing emotions to cloud your ethical judgment.

The German philosopher Immanuel Kant (1724–1804) thought along these lines. He argued that no matter the situation, you should act as if your action could become a universal law for anyone in any situation.

To illustrate this, Kant posed the following thought experiment: Suppose an innocent man is hiding in your house. A murderer trying to kill him knocks on your door, asking if he is there. Should you lie in order to save the innocent man, or should you tell the truth?

Kant's famous answer was that you must always tell the truth, since the injunction not to lie is absolute and should not be altered depending on the situation. The point of his intellectual exercise was to argue that the context of the situation is irrelevant. Even in such an obvious situation where just about any human being would lie (as Kant himself even acknowledged), lying was still the wrong thing to do.

From a pure Kantian perspective, a question like how to help a friend in trouble would never be considered a useful starting point for ethical reflection. It involves too many messy issues: the complexities of your friend's troubles, how vulnerable she is and who else around her is supporting her, her history of dealing with crises, the conflicting emotions of everyone else involved in the situation.

For Confucius, however, the friend-in-trouble scenario is *precisely* the sort of example that prompts us to think about ethical behavior. It's not just that Confucius might say that of course you lie to save the innocent man, since you need to be thinking about the whole situation and not just about a broad moral imperative such as "It is wrong to lie." He would probably believe that by stripping the situation of all the complex details, Kant made his thought experiment fundamentally useless.

Trying to formulate abstract, universal laws to guide us is not only irrelevant but also dangerous. It prevents us from learning how to wrestle with the complexities of situations. It obstructs our understanding how to express goodness.

Confucius would likely remind us that there is a single thing you can do, and one thing only, to help a friend in trouble: bring your sensibility to the situation in order to understand what your friend's real troubles are. Every situation is unique, and it changes from moment to moment; the changes are brought about by everything from whether your friend got enough sleep last night to the way you respond when she's sharing her troubles with you. Your reading of the situation, your ability to grasp the big picture, your capacity to understand all the complex factors that have led your friend to this specific moment in time, are what help you to respond with goodness. You will understand if your friend needs someone to play a more interventionist role ("You've got to get your life together!"); or if she needs a calm, sympathetic confidant ("That sounds hard"); or whether or not it helps if you quietly make her a cup of tea or offer to pick up her dry cleaning.

Most of us know all this, to some extent. But from a Confucian standpoint, we can do it even better. We can understand that no norms can tell us exactly what to do once we are out in the messy world, juggling myriad roles and emotions and scenarios. The only norm is goodness. For Confucius, cultivating and expressing goodness are the only ways to become an ethical person.

Creating and Altering Rituals

Confucius is often stereotyped as a rigid traditionalist who urged his followers to spend their lives following social conventions and fitting into specific roles. But by now, it should be clear that he taught the opposite. As we conduct our rituals and gain a sense of goodness, we become the very opposite of rigid. Not only do rituals help prevent us from becoming stuck in any one role, but also training ourselves in rituals means learning when and how to create or alter them.

In fact, the *Nature That Emerges from the Decree* tells us that rituals originated in just this way. In the earliest days of human civilization, people experienced moments when, amidst the riotous, negative encounters they were having as they bumped up against one another, things actually went well. (Think of something as simple as asking for something rather than just grabbing it, or assisting a friend who was struggling rather than ignoring him.) People took note of the positive effects of these encounters and began to repeat them, and these became rituals. Over time, people developed a repertoire of rituals that helped guide them to behave well toward one another and to help teach future generations to do so as well.

We too create and alter rituals. Imagine that you walk into a room and see that your wife looks concerned about something. In the past, whenever you've seen her in this sort of a state, you've sat down next to her and encouraged her to talk it out. Giving her room to express her feelings has always been the established ritual.

But a Confucian perspective would emphasize the complexities: meaning, in this particular situation, understanding what kind of attention she needs right now. This could mean recognizing that doing something different—just holding her close, silently—is best for her at this moment, because you sense that what she needs most right now is to be reassured by your presence. If you do this, you create a new ritual. You do something new, quite intentionally, based on your experience with the rituals you two have used before, your knowledge of your wife, and your reading of the situation. If this works, she will respond differently in turn, and this will slowly become a ritual between you two. You've altered previous rituals and created a new one. And in doing so, you have created a new reality for the two of you: a reality in which you have forged a better connection.

* * *

If we succeed at expressing goodness continuously, what do we get out of it? At times, Confucius's disciples asked him similar questions. In fact, they asked whether he thought we are rewarded after we die for the good things we do for others. His response was simple:

"You do not yet understand life—how could you understand death?"

Confucius's answer wasn't to say that we should, or should not, believe in an afterlife. Rather, he was emphasizing that we should concentrate on what we can do in the here and now to bring out the best in those around us.

Although Confucius's focus is not on one's own happiness, he was intimately familiar with the deep happiness that comes from striving to become a better human being. When asked to describe himself, he replied:

"He is a person who is so impassioned that he forgets to eat, who is so joyous that he forgets to be worried, and who grows into old age without noticing time passing by."

Cultivating Ourselves to Cultivate a Better World

"Overcoming the self and turning to ritual is how one becomes good."

Remember the history of the please-and-thank-you ritual. What seemed a minor shift several centuries ago eventually became part of something greater. A new world began to develop, one where people could imagine what it would be like to treat one another like equals, and then experience momentarily what it felt like to treat one another equally. Over time, we have become a world where it is generally believed that people should be equal.

We tend to believe that to change the world, we have to think big. Confucius wouldn't dispute this, but he would likely also say, Don't ignore the small. Don't forget the "pleases" and "thank yous." Change doesn't happen until people alter their behavior, and they don't alter their behavior unless they start with the small.

Confucius taught that we can cultivate goodness only through rituals. Yet it is only once we conduct our lives with goodness that we gain a sense of when to employ rituals and how to alter them. This may sound circular, and it is. This very circularity is part of the profundity of his thought. There is no ethical or moral framework that transcends context and the complexity of human life. All we have is the messy world within which to work and better ourselves. These ordinary as-if rituals are the means by which we imagine new realities and over time construct new worlds. Our lives begin in the everyday and stay in the everyday. Only in the everyday can we begin to create truly great worlds.

4

On Decisions: Mencius and the Capricious World

I magine trying to come up with a plan to jump-start your life. Perhaps you're an ambitious college graduate just entering the workforce, or you are stuck in a midlife crisis both personally and professionally. Or maybe you're trying to decide whether to marry your girlfriend, or else you and your spouse want to start a family but aren't sure how to make that work with both of your demanding careers. And then imagine that you embark on your plan, only to run into setback after setback: you send out dozens of résumés, to no avail. Your girlfriend decides she doesn't want to get married after all and breaks up with you. You and your spouse have a baby born with a serious condition that will require intensive full-time care. Despite all your planning, you are faced with unexpected results, and it is crushing.

One of our philosophers experienced something surprisingly similar in his own life. In the late fourth century BC, during an era of strife now known as the Warring States period, Mencius, a Confucian scholar, decided that the time was right for the beginning of a new dynasty based on Confucian teachings. Although already quite an old man, he began going from state to state and talking to their rulers, hoping to persuade one of them to hire him as an advisor, listen to his teachings, and put them into practice.

After many years, the ruler of the state of Qi appointed Mencius to a prominent ministerial position and gave him many audiences. Everything the old philosopher had devoted his entire life to seemed about to come to fruition: he would be the philosopher standing behind a good king and helping him usher in a new and peaceful age.

But it soon became clear that the ruler of Qi was not interested in learning from the scholar's teachings. When the king waged a war against a neighboring state after tricking Mencius into seeming to have urged him to do so, Mencius realized with despair that his work there was done. The king had used him to make his aggressive act appear virtuous and had no intention of listening to him. It was too late for him to go elsewhere. Mencius would never become the philosopher to a worthy ruler. He left Qi and returned to his home.

Mencius faced an all-too human dilemma: a profoundly disappointing setback had wrecked the plans he had laid out so carefully. He railed against his fate. He reproached Heaven.

But the experience shaped his philosophy greatly. Mencius would argue that the very things we believe to be true when we plan out our lives are also the things that, ironically, limit us.

How we live and make decisions comes down to whether we believe we live in a world that is coherent and stable or one that is—as Mencius taught—unpredictable and capricious. But how can we live a good life if we give up the notions that the world is ordered and just and that mapping out our lives is how we attain success? How do we plan for anything, decide on anything, if we live in a capricious world?

Coherent and Capricious Worlds

When we plan for the future, we tend to assume that the future is predictable. Of course, we pay lip service to the notion that life can change on a dime and that nothing is certain. But we're still often taken by surprise when things don't turn out the way we'd expected. And that's because when it comes to how we live our lives, we tend to behave as if there are certain stable factors we can count on in a world that is coherent, and this assumption affects our decisions.

Mozi, one of Mencius's contemporaries, held this worldview. A man of humble birth who made his own way in the world, he eventually founded a tight-knit religious community, and his philosophical writings sketch out his vision of a just society in which anyone who worked hard would prosper.

Mozi shared the Confucian idea that society was failing to enable human flourishing. He too believed people should be encouraged to be ethically better. But unlike the Confucians, Mozi and his followers (the Mohists) didn't believe that rituals were a tool for helping people to become good. Instead, they dismissed them as meaningless and formulaic, a waste of time that prevented people from focusing on what was really important. And what they thought was really important was sincere belief: in this case, to Heaven, or *Tian*, the deity who they believed had created the world.

For Mozi and his followers, Heaven was a moral deity who laid out clear guidelines of right and wrong. Humans had to follow these guidelines in order to live a good life. If they did, they would be rewarded; if they did not, they would be punished. In the current age, Mozi believed, people were failing to follow these guidelines, and this was what was leading to immorality, societal decadence, and political turbulence. The Mohists envisioned rebuilding society modeled on *Tian*'s moral code. Mozi thought that if people were taught to believe that some sort of just, moral code underpinned the universe, this would compel them to behave ethically, resulting in a better society. With their emphasis on sincere belief, their suspicion of ritual, and their commitment to a coherent and predictable world created by a good deity, the Mohists were in many ways quite similar to the early Protestants.

Protestant ideas have helped shape much of what we take for granted now in the modern world. We may or may not still believe in God, but we still believe in the same basic framework. We are stable selves who live in a stable world. We should act as rational-choice agents, calculating what will benefit us and what will cause us harm. If we look within, discover who we are, set out a plan for how we can flourish, and then work hard to fulfill that plan, we will prosper and grow as we should. In short, we are Mohists.

Furthermore, while Confucians thought of goodness as something you couldn't describe in the abstract but as something you understood differently according to each situation you found yourself in, Mozi's notion was abundantly clear: goodness was always whatever benefited the greatest number of people. He declared that how people feel about those they are closest to should not matter, for there should be no gradations of love. Rather, men and women should strive to care for everyone equally. Four centuries later, Jesus preached similarly the virtues of loving thy neighbor, loving thy enemy, and turning the other cheek. And in our own day, we are encouraged to donate to charity, volunteer our services, care for the unfortunate.

Yet of course, Mozi recognized that people didn't naturally behave ethically, and that their emotions and selfish desires got in the way. He believed that society should be set up to nudge people toward correct behavior. These incentives included rewards (success, money, fame) when people did things they should, and punishments (failure, demotions, fines) when they did not. If people believed they lived in a world with clear notions of right and wrong—where hard work would be rewarded and bad deeds punished—they would be persuaded not to follow their baser emotions but to strive to become good people. Mozi was certain that once the right system was in place, the result would be a society in which everyone benefited; a world of what he called "universal caring."

* * *

Mencius disagreed strenuously with Mozi on all of this. At first glance, his stance might seem puzzling: What could possibly be objectionable about a just world where hard work brings prosperity, there are reliable standards of right and wrong, and everyone is cared for equally?

But Mencius held a very different worldview, one rooted in Confucian thought. He saw the world as capricious. Hard work would not necessarily lead to prosperity. Bad deeds would not necessarily be punished. There were no guarantees of anything; no stable, overarching coherence to the world that one could count on. Instead, Mencius believed, the world is fragmented, in perpetual disorder, and in need of constant work. And it is only when we understand that nothing is stable that we can make decisions and live our lives in the most expansive way.

This is an unsettling idea, and we know that even Mencius struggled to accept it. In fact, he is the philosopher whose life and character we know the most about: the *Mencius,* a collection of his teachings compiled by his disciples after his death, is rich in detailed stories, dialogues, and anecdotes that portray him as utterly human. This is what makes the text so compelling: it conveys a sense of what it means to be a fallible human being, in all its complexity. Mencius is no serene Buddha, no selfless Jesus. Far from being a placid and benign wise man, he comes across as a brilliant, mercurial, strong-willed, arrogant, and complicated figure—a man who struggled to achieve goodness and at times failed to live up to his own philosophy.

Given this view of the world as continually knitted together by human actions, Mencius found Mozi's ideas particularly dangerous. He believed that Mozi's ideas would not result in a world of social harmony and universal caring. Instead, they would result in a near Pavlovian world where people had been conditioned to do what they had to in order to gain rewards and avoid punishment. It would be a world, in fact, in which people had been trained to think of their actions purely in terms of self-interest: *What do I do to get what I want?*

In fact, Mencius believed one could only become ethical by *not* thinking there exists any coherent system of rewards and punishments. After all, if you believe one exists, then you will not strive to become a better person; you will act in order to gain benefits for yourself. Mozi's grand social vision of how to create a perfect world of universal caring would, ironically, lead instead to a world filled with selfish profit seekers.

Mencius feared that attempts to shape human behavior in such a calculated way would end up dividing our cognitive thinking from our emotional side. Realistically, how could we ever love a stranger's child as much as our own? Of course, removing our emotions from the equation was precisely Mozi's point: the mind should allow us to decide rationally what's good or not, free of whims and desires. But Mencius believed that what set good people apart from others was that they had not lost touch with their emotional side; instead, they held on to and assiduously cultivated their emotional responses. And that was how they knew the right thing to do—the right decision to make—in any situation.

This philosophical difference between Mozi and Mencius represents the difference between those who see the world as coherent and those who see it as capricious. On the one hand, you have a world in which your actions are shaped by a belief in universally applicable rules; on the other is a world that you can never count on, one that you build anew constantly by cultivating yourself and your relationships through small actions.

How We Decide

Even today, though we hardly realize it, our decisions are shaped by whether we see the world as coherent or capricious. Most of us, like Mozi, see the world as coherent. We know full well that things don't always go according to plan, but we also tend to assume there is a general way the world works: if you work hard, you'll do well in school; if you get a good education, you'll find a job you enjoy; if you marry the love of your life, you'll live happily ever after.

Typically, we rely on two folk models to make decisions, both of which are rooted in this idea that there is some stability in the world.

There's the "rational choice" model: we are rational creatures capable of making decisions logically. We do voluminous research, make lists of pros and cons, and weigh risks and benefits to achieve the best outcomes we can. We carefully think through which class to take, whether to go to graduate school, or whether to accept a job offer in a remote city.

Or else we favor the "gut instinct" model, in which we make decisions based on an intuitive feeling about what feels "right." We decide where to go out for dinner, where to travel on our next vacation, or which couch to buy for the living room.

Ultimately, most of us employ some sort of combination of the two. We do the research, but then go with what feels right.

Given his fealty to the idea that the world is capricious, Mencius would consider both decision-making models to be misguided. If we believe we can decide by calculation alone, we will think we are indeed deciding rationally, but those decisions will be derailed by unconscious factors. This isn't news: plenty of research on decision making concludes that emotions often hijack rational thought.

But that certainly doesn't mean we ought to rely instead on gut instincts, which are often little more than the manifestation of untrained or even selfish desires, and not based on a true sense of the right thing to do.

There's a third approach. We can constantly hone our emotional sense so that it works in sync with our mind, in order to make decisions that open up the future rather than close it down. We do not live in an unchanging world, and that is why the last thing we should do is remove emotions—which allow us to grasp all the nuances of a situation and navigate through it from any starting point.

You will not mend a troubled relationship with your sister by sitting down for a single big breakthrough heart-to-heart talk. It will happen instead through the tiny decisions you make about how to behave and respond every time you talk, even when she's pushing all your buttons. Consider what happens if you shift your focus to examine your everyday interactions with her, while recognizing all the small details (including her responses to your own demeanor) affecting those interactions. Just as the world is not stable, these interactions are not fixed. If you understand that, then you can work simultaneously to alter the situation and the relationship by honing your emotions so that your better responses create a better trajectory.

These possible trajectories exist all around us. When

you put off calling a faraway friend because you are waiting for your yearly get-together to catch up, you are actively choosing not to nourish the friendship. Your neglect is an active choice that will set things on a certain path. If your boyfriend is contemplating breaking up, and you insist anxiously that the two of you hash things out right now—instead of waiting a bit to see how time changes and softens both your emotions—you are hastening along a conclusion that might not have happened otherwise. If you voice a complaint calmly and courteously—let's say that you've asked to speak to the manager of a store where the customer service was poor—you will open up the conversation between the two of you rather than shut it down by becoming angry and loud, and possibly change the outcome for the better.

Remember the dilemma of how to best help a friend in trouble? Typically, we respond based on what we think we can do to help that particular friend in that particular situation. By acknowledging the specificity of the situation, we are indeed behaving in a Confucian way. It would never dawn on most of us to think first about rational benefit and universally applicable norms in this situation.

Yet because we often think of ourselves as being a certain, stable way, we confine ourselves to certain past roles. If you think of yourself as the sympathetic type, for instance, you might be uncomfortable being more overtly interventionist—even if you can see that's what your friend really needs at that moment—because it's just not who you are. It falls outside the pattern of how you usually behave. You might think, *Well, another friend can push her to see a doctor/call the lawyer/confront her coach. I'll just listen.*

But defining yourself as "who you are" limits your sensitivity to the entire situation, the breadth of the response you can give, and the goodness you can show,

In order to sense the whole context before making a decision in an endlessly shifting world, you need to train your emotions. You need to learn what it means to think of decisions in terms of a complex self and a complex world and complex trajectories that can go in multiple directions.

Mencius believed that the only way to cultivate a full awareness of the complexity of situations is by cultivating our ability to understand how our actions can lead to positive trajectories. And he believed we are all born with the potential to do so: a potential for goodness.

Our Potential for Goodness

Imagine for a moment that you are walking through a grassy field where some children are playing. Suddenly, you hear a shriek. A boy has disappeared from sight, slipping into an abandoned well. He is now hanging onto the edge, desperately trying to keep from falling to the bottom.

Without hesitation—without thinking even for an instant—you run to rescue the child. You reach in and heave him out to safety.

Mencius used the parable of the child in the well to

emphasize that all human beings have the same potential to become good. We know this is so, he argued, because there isn't a person anywhere who would not instantly race over to help that child. And the reason for doing so would not be for acclaim, for rewards, or for praise or gratitude from the child's parents. It would be a spontaneous reaction that any human being anywhere would have, and it would spring from a pure desire to simply save that child.

If we could develop this instinct, we *would* know what to do and what to decide in just about any situation. Yet it is hard to live up to our potential for good. We gossip about neighbors, we're jealous of friends, we yell at our children. Over and over, we let our worst sides come to the surface. If we would all run to rescue a child in peril, then why, in our daily lives, do we hurt those around us so often? Why don't we do more to nurture our potential for goodness?

Mencius found this all the more puzzling given his belief that every human being is born with a natural capacity for goodness. He wrote:

The goodness of human nature is like water tending to flow downward. Just as there is no water that does not flow downward, there are no humans who do not have goodness.

But this goodness exists only *in potentia*. Human nature is potentially good, but it can be lost, it can be warped, it can be changed by what it encounters. As Mencius said:

*You can dam and direct the water, and you can force
it to remain on the top of a mountain without flowing down. But is this what water's nature really is? It
is what you have done to it that makes it so. Humans
can also be made to be not good in the same way.*

Mencius wanted people to understand viscerally the sensation of goodness in order to understand how to become
good. What does it physically feel like to be good? What
do you do on a daily basis to gain that feeling?

To answer these questions, Mencius taught that we
should think of our incipient goodness as being like small
sprouts. All sprouts have the potential to grow into something greater. But they must be cultivated properly in a
nurturing environment to achieve that potential. Similarly,
each of us has incipient goodness within us, and so each of
us, Mencius concluded, begins life endowed equally with
the potential to become like a sage: capable of creating an
environment in which everyone will flourish.

But we tend to either neglect our sprouts, forgetting to
water or nourish them, or else we are too forceful: we grab
them and try to tug at them to make them grow. Not only
do we disrupt our natural goodness, but also we become
miserable, easily dominated by our worst instincts: jealousy, anger, and resentment. When we do this, we harm
our own humanity and harm those around us. By unleash-
ing the worst in ourselves, we bring out the worst in others
and cause them to kill their sprouts too. Most of us fail to
achieve our potential, but this is not how it has to be.

If goodness is indeed as physically perceivable as actual sprouts are, then it is not something abstract, like Mohist universal caring or Buddhist universal compassion; it is not linked to any sort of doctrine that requires us to feel the same toward strangers we've never even met as we do toward lifelong friends. Rather, goodness is something we can feel and nurture in our everyday lives with the very people we're with right now.

If we pay attention whenever we perform an act of kindness, no matter how small—speaking to someone warmly, holding open a door for strangers, helping neighbors shovel out their cars after a snowstorm—we might experience a physical sensation such as warmth or a tiny glow. That concrete sensation is Mencius's sprout of goodness growing within, nurtured by our act of generosity and connection to another.

As you pay attention to that physical feeling, nurture the better sides of yourself, and notice the impact on yourself and on others, you become motivated to continue. In this way, you are not growing your goodness in the abstract: you are learning through every step of this process how to sow the conditions in which it can thrive. You begin as a lone farmer, cultivating your sprouts in your humble field, but the effect radiates outward. Those on the receiving end of our goodness become inspired to act better and to continue growing their own sprouts of goodness in turn. Such moments of goodness build until they fill a day, and eventually an entire life.

The Heart-Mind as One

How is goodness related to making sound decisions?

We bring out the great potential of human nature when we perfect our emotional responses. Continuously cultivating ourselves through our interactions with others and constantly working on nourishing our sprouts of goodness—these are what lead us ultimately to understand how to make the right moral decision in any given situation.

Although some thinkers like Mozi believed in making a clear distinction between the rational and emotional faculties and separating the mind and the heart as much as possible, in Chinese, the word for *mind* and *heart* is actually one and the same: *xin*. The heart-mind is the seat of our emotions as well as the center of our rationality. It can deliberate, ponder, contemplate, and feel love, joy, and hatred. What separates those who become great human beings from those who do not, Mencius taught, is the capacity to follow their heart-mind rather than to go along blindly with either the senses or the intellect. Cultivating the heart-mind is what fosters our ability to decide well.

Think of the choices we are faced with throughout life, from the prosaic to the profound: what to make for dinner; where to go on your next vacation; whether to switch jobs; or whether to file for divorce. Wise decisions don't come just from thinking things through rationally. They come from a complete understanding of what our heart-mind knows is the right thing to do. Good decisions are made when mind and heart are integrated.

When we are passively led by our senses, we make unwise and unbridled decisions. Whether it's something minor, such as overeating when we're not that hungry, or something more significant, like heatedly berating a partner for a perceived slight, our senses often mislead us into reacting unwisely in the moment.

But if we have cultivated our heart-mind, we respond to things from a far more stable place. Undistracted by impulses and by emotional swings, we can focus on the big picture and know what to do. We know which responses bring out the best in us and in those around us.

Let's return to the story of the child in the well. This parable describes, of course, a rare moment of crisis. But most decisions we face in life are not as clear-cut. A latent inclination for goodness will not immediately tell us what to do. It tells us, of course, that we need to save the boy. But how, exactly, should you best help a cousin dealing with a personal crisis? Which job offer would be right for your future? Should you move home to be closer to your ailing parents?

A Mencian approach to integrating your cognitive and emotional sides would be to take note of your emotional responses and then strive to change them for the better. Use your mind to cultivate your emotions. Become aware of what triggers your emotions and reactions on a daily basis. What are the patterned habits, the entrenched narratives, through which you perceive the world? Does your partner's criticizing you for the way you load the dishwasher trigger memories of your own childhood, when you were constantly made to feel inept? Do you tend to placate friends instead of being assertive because you feel unworthy of expressing a strong opinion?

As you become aware of all the triggers and old patterns that shape your emotions throughout the day, you can work on refining your responses. Note that paying attention to your emotional responses is not the same as "mindfulness," the popular notion that is based loosely on the Buddhist idea of detachment and nonjudgment. It is not about observing your feelings, accepting them, and then letting them go so that you can achieve a sort of personal peace. Because even if you did achieve a peaceful feeling, it would disappear soon after you started to engage with the world again. Nor is it about feeling compassion for all beings in an abstract way. Cultivating the heart-mind is an outwardly directed act intended not to remove us from the world but to engage us more deeply in it so we can better ourselves and those around us through every interaction. It's about paying attention not in a mindful sense but in a Confucian one.

External events trigger our emotional responses every day, like the surge of joy you feel when your toddler spontaneously brings you a bunch of flowers he picked just for you, the flash of pain you feel running into an ex-love on the street, the jolt of anxiety you feel when your boss sends you an email reminding you about an upcoming deadline. All our responses accumulate. Life becomes a series of untrained patterned responses—patterns that often end up being negative. In fact, a lot of what we tend to think of as conscious decision making *is* just us playing out old patterns. But if we cultivate our emotions, over time and with experience, we can learn to sense other people's dispositions more accurately, assess what's really going on in a particular situation, and work to shift the outcome accordingly—whether we are dealing with a conflict with a neighbor, a friend who is struggling with depression, or a child who's falling behind at school. We can train ourselves to remain ever aware of these complexities and to know what we can do to alter them.

Imagine that you have a coworker who interrupts you incessantly whenever you're on a deadline. This chronic problem has caused you to form an idea of her as oblivious and annoying. You might feel tempted to give her the cold shoulder. Or you might give in and chat with her but then be annoyed with yourself for having let her take up so much of your time. Or you might blow up at her, furious that she doesn't realize how busy you are. Or you might vent to your friends, who urge you to assert yourself and tell her in no uncertain terms that you cannot talk to her right now. But rather than label her and employ generic strategies aimed at a generic annoying, interrupting coworker, the most expansive response comes when you begin to recognize your coworker as an individual with a complex set of sensibilities, habits, patterns, emotions, and behaviors. Certain sides of her are playing out in this given situation for certain reasons, just as certain sides of you are. You might feel tempted to address the issue head-on and tell her you have a problem that the two of you need to discuss in order to get her to recognize your position. But the more efficient strategy will be to understand how altering things that *you* do will alter the direction of this situation over time. Once you see her as multifaceted and infinitely complex, rather than as a unified person who just is the way she is, it opens up your perspective to various things you can try to alter the situation; small things you can do to draw out different sides of your coworker, as well as yourself. Does she come to talk when she is lonely? Might there be other ways to address her desire for interaction? Or maybe she keeps checking in when she's feeling uncertain and insecure; addressing the nervousness itself is where you might begin.

Here's another situation: let's say that someone treats you with anger. Maybe a long-simmering resentment between you and your brother has finally exploded into the open. A refined response would be not to automatically respond with anger of your own—tempting though it might be. Nor would it be to placate him, numb out, or simply avoid talking. Rather, a refined response begins by taking a moment to try to grasp all the emotions and triggers that lie behind your brother's behavior. There is the immediate catalyst, of course, but the current state of the relationship has almost certainly built up over years of patterned responses—on both your parts. If you start by trying to sense where the anger comes from and to grasp what might be done to alter those pieces of the situation, you will be lifted out of the mind-set that has you thinking of him as just being a certain way. New approaches will occur to you. Small gestures (as simple as an acknowledgment of anger, an admission of your own role in it, or a measured decision to wait to talk until the two of you have cooled down), precisely because they are counterintuitive and are directed at changing the underlying dynamic rather than responding heatedly to the immediate issue, have the capacity to break that underlying dynamic.

None of these ideas is new to us: we know these are optimal ways to respond. And yet a refined response is not usually the first reaction we have when responding to highly challenging interpersonal situations. Most of us are usually buffeted about by the emotions of the moment and a desire for quick resolution. This different approach certainly offers no quick fix; none of this changes things immediately. But you accumulate experience in thinking of things in terms of the big picture; the long-term outcome. When you make a point of training yourself to approach situations with the broadest perspective and an understanding of how to alter an outcome, you are constantly cultivating your potential for goodness. This is not about overriding our emotions, because that would cause us to lose our ability to sense the overall context of a situation. It is about refining those emotions so that the better response comes to the fore intuitively.

This is what it means to cultivate the heart-mind. It allows you to become more responsive to the world, your better sides to remain intact, and your vision to remain unimpaired. What Mencius referred to as "flexible judgment" is the ability to make good moral decisions instinctively while carefully weighing each situation in all its complexity. Training our heart-mind means honing our judgment: seeing the bigger picture, understanding what really lies behind a person's behavior, and remembering that different emotions such as anxiety, fear, and joy will draw out different sides of people we tend to think of as rigid. A sense for the right thing to do becomes a more complex, developed form of the instinct that would compel you to save a child in a well. Just as you wouldn't have to ask yourself consciously what to do about a child in peril, you wouldn't have to ask yourself how to move through life's daily encounters if you had nurtured the heart-mind.

Laying the Ground So Things Can Grow

When it comes to larger life decisions—which college major to choose, whether to switch careers, whom to marry—we often make a mistake. Even if we use our heart-mind to make flexible judgments and recognize how our actions create small changes in the world constantly, we still think of the world as coherent, and thus we persist in thinking that there are some stable things: *me, my strengths and weaknesses, my likes and dislikes, the world as it will be decades hence and my position in it.*

Thus, not just our short-term responses but also our long-term life plans are often based on an illusion of stability. We plan out what we can do concretely to get ourselves to our goals. If you are trying to decide on a career, for instance, you might think through what would suit you best: you figure out what kind of person you are, where your strengths lie, focus on classes and pursuits based on that assessment, and, finally, embark on a career path based on this fixed definition of who you believe you are.

But remember that who you think you are—and especially what you think is "you" when you are making decisions—is usually just a set of patterns you've fallen into. Just as you can become a pessimistic person simply because you think of yourself as pessimistic, you can make decisions that shape who you become, just because you think they reflect who you are. But when you do this, you box yourself in before you've even begun.

When we rationally make big life decisions based on the idea that the world is coherent, we assume a clear-cut situation, clear-cut possibilities, a stable self, unchanging emotions, and an unchanging world. But these things aren't givens at all. By making concrete, defined plans, you are actually being abstract, because you are making these plans for a self that is abstract: a future self that you imagine based on who you think you are now, even though you, the world, and your circumstances will change. You cut yourself off from the real, messy complexities that are the basis from which you can develop as a human being. You eliminate your ability to grow as a person because you are limiting that growth to what is in the best interests of the person you happen to be right now, and not the person you will become.

If, instead, you maintain a constant consciousness of the world as unstable, you can start to think of all your decisions and responses as based on an awareness of the complex, ever-changing world and your complex, ever-shifting self. You can train your mind to stay open and take into account all the complex stuff that is you. We achieve the best outcomes when we think of things in terms of long-term trajectories. The most expansive decisions come from laying the ground so things can grow.

Consider this story from the *Mencius,* a tale about the sage kings of old who ushered in the dawn of civilization. It was a time when "all under Heaven was not yet regulated, flooding waters flowed throughout, and the five grains did not grow."

The sage king Yu was sent to put this world in order. He dug the earth and provided irrigation for crops:

Yu dredged the nine rivers, cleaned out the Ji and Ta so that they flowed into the sea, cleared the Ru and Han, and opened the Huai and Si so that they flowed into the Jiang. Only then were the people of the central states able to obtain food.

Bo Gui said: "My method of regulating the water is superior to that of Yu." Mencius said: "You are wrong. Yu's method of regulating the water was based on the way of the water. It is for this reason that Yu used the four seas as the receptacle. But you are using the neighboring states as the receptacle. When water goes contrary to its course, we call it overflowing water. Overflowing water means flooding water, something that a humane man detests. You are wrong. . . .

"As for Yu's moving the waters, he moved them without interference."

Yu made radical changes to the environment by digging ditches and channels, but he also made these changes after understanding how the water flowed and moved naturally.

The point of the story is not that we should passively allow water to flow as it will, just as we should not passively allow sprouts to grow as they might. It's that we must be like Yu channeling the waters. We must be like a farmer cultivating his crops. A farmer is active and deliberate. He chooses the right spot, pulls up the weeds, turns and fertilizes the soil, and sows his crops—ones that he knows already will flourish in that particular climate. He then cultivates his field, weeding it, nurturing the growing plants with water, and making sure they get enough sunlight. But the work doesn't even end there. It is constant. He builds fences to keep out wild animals and shifts his crops depending on the altering nature of the soil. He is also keenly sensitive to timing and pacing: he knows when to make changes and when to wait. In life we want to constantly be ever-responsive to new circumstances as they arise, just as a farmer is vigilant about situations that affect his field.

Being active does not mean aggressively trying to dam up flowing water. Instead, it is like taking advantage of the fact that water tends to flow downward to help you manage that water. As Mencius said, "What I dislike about crafty people is that they chisel their way through. If they were instead like the sage king who moved the waters, then there would be nothing to dislike. The sage king who moved the waters moved them without interference."

Being active consists of creating optimal conditions and responding to whatever various situations arise. It means laying the ground in which change can grow. Think of yourself as a farmer, rather than thinking about who you are and arranging your goals around that. Your goal then becomes laying the ground for various interests and sides of yourself to grow organically.

Most of us have hobbies and interests we pursue on the weekend or in our free time. We often don't think of those things as relevant to figuring out what we want to do with our life. And yet laying the ground means something as simple as scheduling time to take part in activities that speak to the different sides of yourself that you are interested in developing: joining a wine tasting class, learning how to paint in watercolor, or brushing up on your high school French once a week in a language swap. By proactively building room in your life for all sorts of possibilities, and then remaining open and responsive, you are akin to a farmer preparing his field so that his crops can flourish.

As you make room for interests, opportunities open up to you. You might learn that you love working with your hands, but would rather try woodworking than painting. Or you decide that French isn't for you, but you want to explore other cultures by offering to tutor immigrants at the public library instead, which could eventually lead to other things: new friends, a trip abroad, a change of career down the road. By being responsive to how your interests change over time, you will not be locked in—you will be more able to alter your life and your schedule to allow for growth.

Rather than going into all of this thinking, *I can be anything I want to be,* the approach you're taking is *I don't know yet what I can become.* You don't know where any of this might take you; it's not possible to know that now. But what you learn about yourself and what excites you won't be abstract; it will be very concrete knowledge born of practical experience. Over time, you open up paths that you could not have imagined, out of which emerge options that you never would have seen before. Over time, you actually become a different person.

You can't plan out how everything in your life will play out. But you can think in terms of creating the conditions in which things will likely move in certain directions: the conditions that allow for the possibility of rich growth. By doing all this, you are not just being a farmer. You are also the results of the farmer's work. You become the fruit of your labor.

Ming and the Unpredictability of Life

Despite all that you do to keep your life open and to stay responsive, things don't always turn out well. You can apply for a job, do the very best you can during interviews, and be rejected in the last round. You can pour your heart into a relationship, only to be dumped. You can arrange to take off six months from work in order to travel, only to learn that your father is critically ill and that you need to cancel your trip to spend time with him in his final months. This is the sort of world that Mencius envisioned, very different from that of the Mohists.

In Mencius's world, *ming* prevails. *Ming* has been translated variously as Heaven's commands, fate, or destiny. But for Mencius, it was a term for the contingency of life: the events, good and bad, that happen outside our control. *Ming* explains that windfalls (such as a job opening) and tragedies (such as a death) happen no matter what we have planned or intended.

We know *ming*: Talented people get fired and can't find another job. The person we love decides, inexplicably, to leave us. Good friends die suddenly, leaving behind young, grieving children. Confucius's favorite disciple died tragically young. Mencius, you'll recall, suffered a major personal crisis late in life, when the ruler of Qi took advantage of him. He struggled to accept the fact that we cannot control the events that affect us deeply. The best plans, the most carefully made decisions, never guarantee against arbitrary, sometimes tragic, events.

When we assume that the world is stable, it leads us down one of two culturally sanctioned roads: belief in either fate or free will. A fatalist might think that whatever happened was meant to be, whether ordained by a deity or by fate; she'd work to accept the ways of the universe. Someone who believes in free will thinks that he controls his own destiny and might have trouble letting himself be touched by tragedy. In the face of, say, a career setback, divorce, or death, he might crumble under feelings of responsibility, or he might be steely and move on as quickly as possible. All of the above are passive reactions because they deny the unpredictability of life.

But Mencius said of *ming*: "It should never be anyone's fate to die in shackles."

Dying in shackles means failing to respond properly to what befalls us. It means letting our reaction be controlled by the things that happen to us. Whether we let tragedies destroy us or we accept what happened, both of these responses are the equivalent of standing under a falling wall and then saying it was your fate to be killed by that wall.

There's another way to respond, one that allows us to

shape our own *ming* and forge our own future. As Mencius tells us, "One who really understands his *ming* does not stand beneath a falling wall. One who dies after fulfilling his way has corrected his destiny."

Living in a capricious world means accepting that we do not live within a stable moral cosmos that will always reward people for what they do. We should not deny that real tragedies do happen. But at the same time, we should always expect to be surprised and learn to work with whatever befalls us. If we can continue this work, even when tragedies come our way, we can begin to accept the world as unpredictable and impossible to determine perfectly. And this is where the promise of a capricious world lies: if our world is indeed constantly fragmented and unpredictable, then it is something we can constantly work on bettering. We can go into each situation resolved to be the best human being we can be, not because of what we'll get out of it, but simply to affect others around us for the better, regardless of the outcome. We can cultivate our better sides and face this unpredictable world, transforming it as we go.

It's a very different vision from asking grand questions such as "Who am I?" and "How should I plan out my life?" Instead, we work constantly to alter things at a small, daily level, and if we're successful, we can build tremendous communities around us in which people can flourish. And even then, we continue to work. Our work—of bettering oneself and others to produce a better world—is never over.

In the face of fate, we should neither feel destroyed nor simply look on the bright side. The cult of positive thinking assures us that whatever difficult circumstances we find ourselves in, it will all work out. But the danger with that position is that it makes us passive. Things will happen that we can't control, but we have a choice to act: to get out of the way of the falling wall, to respond to our *ming* and shape our future accordingly.

Ming is not just about the tragedies that befall us. It's about the good things, too; the unexpected opportunities, unforeseen chances to do something we love, the chance encounter with someone who will change the trajectory of our whole life. When you hold too tightly to a plan, you risk missing out on these things. And when you wake up one day in that future, you will feel boxed in by a life that, at best, reflects only a piece of who you thought you were at one moment in time.

When we can let go of the idea that there are clear guidelines and a stable world, then what we are left with is the heart-mind to guide us. The heart-mind is all there is, and we develop it every day through our relationships with the people we're with. It helps us to sense things correctly, to lay the groundwork for growth, and to work with what we have. And as you do so, all that you thought you were will begin to change. You will find parts of yourself you didn't know existed. The world you once thought of as stable starts instead to seem like a world of infinite possibilities.

5

On Influence: Laozi and Generating Worlds

Imagine you are walking through a forest. It's a glorious summer afternoon, and the sun is shining brightly through the vibrant green leaves. Off in the distance, you see a mighty oak towering above the others. It's so high that you can barely see the top. A few yards away is a tiny sapling, growing in the shadow of the larger tree. Odds are, you will see the larger tree as powerful, steadfast, magisterial, and the sapling as fragile and vulnerable.

But when a windstorm comes, the forest floor will be littered with large branches. The oak tree might not be able to withstand the wind, rain, and lightning of a fierce storm. In the end, it will topple to the ground, yet the sapling will remain intact. Why? The sapling has been bending and shifting with the winds; pliable and soft, it stands up again when the storm has passed. Its very weakness is what has allowed it to flourish and prevail.

* * *

We often assume—because this is what we've been taught—that to be influential we have to be strong and powerful like the tall oak in the forest. We have to assert ourselves convincingly and even bend other people to our will.

But there is another recipe for influence to be found in Chinese philosophical texts such as the *Laozi*, also known as the *Dao de jing*. It derives from appreciating the power of seeming weakness, understanding the pitfalls of differentiation, and seeing the world as interrelated. Rather than think that power comes from strength prevailing over strength, we can understand that true power comes from understanding the connections between disparate things, situations, and people. All of this comes from an understanding of what the *Laozi* calls the *Dao*, or "the Way." The sapling prevails because it is close to the Way.

But a sapling, in the end, is just a sapling. It sways with the wind and grows without consciousness. We human beings can do far more. We are capable of not just understanding connections but also making new ones to generate entirely new realities and new worlds. Being the architects of these worlds is how we become powerful.

Laozi and the Way

Laozi, the Chinese thinker to whom the *Laozi* is attributed, is a mysterious figure. We don't know when he lived, and there is debate over whether Laozi was even the name of a real person. *Laozi* in Chinese simply means "old master," a generic term that could refer to anyone. But in later eras, people attempted to define the author of this compelling text. He was eventually portrayed as a great sage who lived even before Confucius; some wild tales said he lived for three hundred years, and others even claimed that he eventually traveled to India, where he was known as the Buddha. Laozi would also come to be known as the founder of a school of thought—and later an entire religious movement—called Daoism. One legend portrays Laozi as an actual deity, a god who made the cosmos and whose revelations eventually became the *Laozi*.

But Laozi did not found Daoism: the very term "Daoism" was not coined until several centuries after the *Laozi* was written. The reason Laozi was retrospectively considered to have been the founder of Daoism is because of the text's frequent references to the Way.

Most of us, if we have heard of the Way, have some vague notions about what it is. Think of a Chinese landscape painting: brush and ink deftly paint an image of mist-covered mountains dotted subtly with trees and the occasional person, almost too small to see: a pilgrim who has taken solace in the vastness of the natural world. In the West, we tend to interpret these paintings as representative of a human quest to leave society and seek harmony in nature. These paintings appear to portray an unchanging world to which humans must adjust to achieve inner calm and tranquility.

This is how the Way is commonly perceived: as an ideal that is "out there"; the natural perfection that exists beyond us and with which we need to come back into harmony. For many people, the *Laozi* seems to hearken back to a semimythical "golden age," when life was purer and simpler and people were like the pilgrim in the painting: in sync with the natural world, able to flow with things as they were, and close to the Way.

This interpretation, though, dates from the nineteenth century, when the West declared itself modern and the East as its foil. It has more to do with our modern-day romanticizing about what we consider to be traditional Chinese notions about harmony and tranquility than it does with the content of the *Laozi* itself.

The *Laozi* is not telling us that we should simply follow some harmonious pattern that is somewhere "out there" and that we could better reach by going on a pilgrimage or returning to the ways of primitive antiquity. It is not telling us that we should strive to be accepting and tranquil. It teaches a very different notion: that the Way is something we can actively generate ourselves, in the here and now. We each have the potential to become effective and influential in transforming the worlds in which we live. We can re-create the Way.

Re-creating the Way

For Laozi, the Way is the original, ineffable, undifferentiated state that precedes everything. It is:

a thing inchoate and complete,
born before Heaven and earth.

It is that from which everything in the cosmos emerges and to which everything in the cosmos returns.

And it exists on many levels. On an earthly level, the Way is akin to the ground. Think of a blade of grass, growing from the earth. As it grows, it becomes more distinct and differentiated, and as it grows taller, it becomes further separated from the Way. This is why a sapling is closer to the Way than a mature oak tree. But when all these things that grow from the earth die, they return once more to the earth, or the Way:

The myriad things become active
And I thereby watch them return.
Things are teeming and multifarious,
But each returns to its root.

On a more cosmic level, the Way is akin to what modern physicists would say existed before the Big Bang, before the stars and galaxies emerged and the cosmos became differentiated. It was after the Big Bang that the cosmos became a series of differentiated elements governed by laws of space, time, and causality. These are laws that appear natural to us and that we cannot change or control. This is a universe that we must simply live in. At some point, the theory goes, all these differentiated things will revert back to nothingness once more.

But at the grandest level of all, the *Laozi* concentrates on where everything, at every moment, comes from before it becomes differentiated. It compares the Way to a mother who gives birth to "the myriad things"—meaning everything in the universe. Everything in the universe starts out soft and supple when it comes into existence. Those myriad things, when they first arise, are like children. Like a sapling or a blade of grass, they are soft and supple because they are still so close to the Way. But as time passes, they become more rigid and differentiated from everything else.

The more we see the world as differentiated, the more removed we become from the Way. The more we see the world as interconnected, the closer we come to the Way. We gain power by becoming closer to the Way because we can harness the power of suppleness and weakness.

We cannot generate new natural laws for the universe. But the Way is not just about things happening at a cosmic level. At the most mundane level of our everyday lives, new situations emerge constantly, and each is like a miniature world emerging out of the Way. If we understand the process of things emerging from the Way, then instead of simply living within all these situations and worlds, we can gain the power to alter them. In our social worlds, we can successfully generate new interactions, circumstances, and understandings.

When we understand how to do this, we can become more than a child; we can become like the mother. We give birth to new realities:

All under Heaven had a beginning.
It can be taken as the mother of all under Heaven.
Once you have obtained the mother,
you can thereby know the sons.
Once you have known the sons, you can return and
  hold fast to the mother.
Until the end there will be no harm.

Instead of merely being one of the myriad elements floating about in the universe, when we understand how the world works, we can actually gain the power to re-create the Way all the time, at every moment.

False Distinctions

To re-create the Way in all the situations in our lives, we must recognize the degree to which the distinctions that pervade our experience are actually false. For instance, many people who are familiar with Asian philosophies learn that they advocate a sort of separation or detachment; that in order to achieve mystical enlightenment, say, we need to leave our normal lives behind and head off into the mountains. Only when we are free of our worldly existence can we achieve oneness with the Way as we meditate our way to inner bliss and self-understanding. Perhaps you have a friend who went on a ten-day silent meditation retreat. Perhaps you have long wanted to escape your life and trek the Appalachian Trail. Perhaps you look forward to a long walk on the beach or your weekly yoga class. But those of us who take hikes, go on retreats, and enjoy meditating all have to return eventually to our normal lives, leaving behind our brief feeling of deeper connectedness to the world.

Most of us inhabit such drastically different realms—work and leisure, professional and personal, mystical and practical, weekday and weekend—that it's not surprising that we see our lives as divided. A weekend walk in the woods feels completely divorced from office work on Monday morning. Though the weekend breaks rejuvenate us, and the effects even linger for a time, they exist in a realm outside of the real life of our workweek.

But by dividing up life and by believing that these aspects of our lives are unrelated to one another, we restrict what we are capable of doing and becoming. The *Laozi* would say that not only are mystical enlightenment and our everyday lives related, but that by separating them, we have fundamentally misunderstood both.

Although we think that taking a rejuvenating weekend walk in the woods is how we reconnect with the world and with ourselves, this attitude leads us to greater disconnection from both. We need to think of our weekday life differently. The Way isn't something we reach while walking in the woods on the weekend. It's something we bring about actively through our daily interactions.

We make distinctions in other realms of our lives as well. Our ambitions and goals often lead us to see ourselves in competition with those around us, separating us from them. Or we may hold strong moral convictions; our certainty that we are absolutely correct in our views on organized religion or standardized testing, abortion or euthanasia can make us less receptive to other people's perspectives, putting up insurmountable walls between ourselves and others.

Again, making distinctions of any sort goes against the Way. As the *Laozi* teaches, there are dangers in distinctions, even those that appear moral and right:

When the great Way is discarded,
    there is goodness and propriety.
When wisdom and cleverness emerge,
    there is great artifice.

The *Laozi* is so committed to rejecting all distinctions that it regards even canonical Confucian tenets—goodness, wisdom—as dangerous because of how they immediately call forth distinctions. To aspire to goodness means to acknowledge immediately the possibility of its opposite existing in the world as well. This sort of thinking leads us away from the Way, a state in which everything is interrelated, with no distinctions.

We even tend to read the *Laozi* itself in a disconnected, differentiated way. It is hugely popular, one of the most widely translated works in the world, and yet people almost invariably read it many different ways: as a great text of mystical philosophy, or a political strategy text teaching the secrets of great leaders, or a martial arts manifesto, or a business guide. Even though each of these interpretations is accurate in a sense, all are limited. If you read the text as a great work of mystical philosophy, you focus on mystical-sounding passages about the Way and ignore the passages about how to become an effective leader. If you read the book as a guide to becoming a great leader, you dismiss passages such as "The spirit of the valley does not die" as perplexing and irrelevant. After all, isn't becoming a mystical sage completely incompatible with becoming a great leader?

But to read the *Laozi* solely as a guide about leadership or a mystical text is to see only part of the picture. A mystical sage and a leader are not actually two separate things. The mystical sage is also an effective leader; the effective leader, a mystical sage. If we don't read these seemingly disparate passages as interrelated, we are missing a crucial part of the *Laozi*'s argument: that we are most effective when we refrain from seeing this text, ourselves, and the world as separated and distinct.

We can try to grasp cognitively the idea of connectedness, but how exactly does avoiding false dichotomies work in practice? Consider these exceedingly mundane examples in which, without realizing it, we are doing something Laozian.

Imagine you are dealing with a difficult supervisor at work: someone who is demanding and mercurial. He seems to have irrational expectations of you and yet doesn't provide you with the guidance or feedback you need. But if you start by trying to figure out what lies behind his behavior toward you, you can think about how to shift the entire relationship in a different direction. Even if he is acting arrogantly or demeaningly toward you, for example, this is often motivated by insecurity. By quietly observing the bigger picture, you can think through whether there is something about you that draws out that insecurity: maybe you have a skill he is feeling competitive about or a weakness he feels he can exploit. What might you be doing unwittingly that feeds into that dynamic, and how can you do it differently? You might notice he is particularly grudging or difficult after you've given a great presentation—even if it's one he had assigned you. But, of course, holding yourself back so he doesn't feel threatened is not the answer. To continue doing well without playing into his competitiveness, before your next presentation, you could try seeking his advice on some small aspect of it, so that he sees you as someone looking to learn from his greater experience. Things like this help you slowly and deliberately shift the relationship over time, making him feel less like an older person in danger of being usurped by a sharp and promising subordinate, and more like an experienced mentor helping a colleague to flourish and grow.

Or say you are a parent, and your three children are home from school on a snow day. Two of them are squabbling, and the atmosphere in your living room is tense. You could urge them to be nice as you talk them through their dispute. You could offer them a bribe or distraction, or simply send them to their rooms. But instead of responding directly to the quarreling—a strategy that would immediately call forth distinctions and create divisions—you can be effective if you work to understand what's happening among everyone, and then shift the attitude of the room to alter what's going on. This means looking past the presenting emotions (the irritation and crankiness) to understand the underlying emotions causing all this to happen: maybe your daughter is acting out because she misses her friends at school, or your son feels ignored because you were distracted all morning. You take a deep breath and then use your calm demeanor, the soft inflections of your voice, and reassuring body language to create a different atmosphere. When you get down at their level and really grasp what they are feeling, it becomes easier to begin to understand what you could do to elicit a different side of one child that will in turn alter the dynamic between him and the others. You become able to address the entire context behind the situation.

Or maybe you have a teenager who has been shutting you out. You're wondering how to be more influential in his life without being overbearing, which would only drive him further away. If he feels the connection between you, instead of seeing the two of you as being at odds with each other, he will respond more to you. By being conscious of the need to build that connection over time in order to have any influence at all, you will start to become aware of what you can do: texting him more often; having casual, nonjudgmental conversations about the music he's into; or making time regularly to do something he really enjoys. You are introducing new rituals in the Confucian sense: as-if rituals that alter this unhealthy dynamic and provide opportunities for the two of you to relate to each other differently. In doing so, you are creating a new status quo for your interactions. What you are doing is Laozian in that no one else is aware of what you have done. The break should feel seamless.

When your aim is to reconnect disparate things, emotions, and people instead of addressing the overt problem directly, you begin to sense how to change the environment and the relationship both at this moment and in the long term. You understand better what it might take to forge a workable relationship with your capricious boss, bring out the connections between your squabbling children, or start to reach your distant teenage son. If you had approached all these situations thinking primarily about a tactic to address the problem directly, you would have missed the answer. Your actions—confronting, coaxing, bribing, scolding, cajoling, being overbearing or intrusive—would have created distinctions between you and those you were dealing with, pitting you in a power struggle that would have deepened divisions.

Of course, all this is common sense. We know that going head-to-head with difficult people rarely results in better relationships with them. We know that sound parenting techniques include calming down, calming others down, and not allowing your own stress to increase the stress already there. But the reason a Laozian approach works is not just that you are being less overt or that everyone is calming down. It works because you are actively reconnecting things, these disparate people, in new ways. These different connections you're making create a different environment. You are smoothing over the distinctions that had divided you from others.

Certain factors govern how people act in a given situation. Understanding them gives you a certain degree of influence by helping you to grasp the whole situation, but even more power comes from being the one who starts generating new situations altogether. Other people then act within the scenario you have created, not realizing that you generated it.

Remember that for Laozi, everything emerges from the Way. By helping to generate certain outcomes around you, you are not merely following the Way. By resetting the attitude of the room and recalibrating the relationships in your life, you literally become the Way.

Strength Lies in Weakness

Weakness overcomes strength,
Softness overcomes hardness.

When we persist in perceiving the world as a collection of completely disparate things (this room, that dog, my cup, your book, you, me, them), we alienate ourselves from the Way. If, on the contrary, we sense how everything is interrelated and recognize that everything we do immediately impacts others, we become more effective. Once we understand how everything is interconnected and appreciate how, paradoxically, there is more power in weakness, we understand the workings of influence.

This might be disconcerting; after all, our culture places such a premium on strength and ambition. It's no surprise that we end up believing at some level that the most effective way to "get ahead" is to get ahead of the next person. Without at least some competitiveness, we worry we will get left behind.

Here again we tend to fall into a false dichotomy: ambition versus passivity, will and strength versus weakness. In fact, although many who read the *Laozi* think it's telling us to get rid of all ambition and be passive and weak, that's not the case at all.

The *Laozi* is very much in favor of effecting change, but it provides an alternative way to fulfill it. The way we typically manifest ambitiousness is by imposing our will. This leads us to overreach, focus on the wrong things, and create the conditions for our own downfall. Our view of ambition and the way we usually pursue it is actually our undoing.

When you're blustering about, when you're trying to gain power by imposing your will on others, it's not that you'll fail. You may succeed, even for a long time. But the degree to which you can succeed is based only upon the amount of actual overt power you have over people to make them cave in. In the end, they will be deeply resentful and will seek ways to try to break your power. Perhaps most important, it takes only one person who understands the real nature of power to overthrow you. It took only one Mohandas Gandhi to end the British Empire, in 1947.

Think of Rosa Parks, the forty-two-year-old woman from Montgomery, Alabama, who, in 1955, at the end of a long day working at a department store, refused to give up her seat on the bus to a white passenger. As Parks recalled, a sudden determination covered her "like a quilt on a winter night," and she chose that moment to refuse to move. This one person understood not just that the time was right to act. She sensed how a quiet response would be more effective than an aggressive one. Her strategy—to sit quietly—inspired fellow community activists to gather behind her in a movement toward equality.

Think of who is most effective in the workplace: the office bully who is always throwing around his weight, trying to dominate everyone else, or the one who is attuned to people's emotions, to how they receive things, who uses humor and laughter to connect, and who stays ever aware of the atmosphere of the place. Think back on the teachers you had as a child. Who was most effective in the classroom: the teacher who used a loud voice and threats to intimidate everyone? Or the one who kept the classroom ticking along harmoniously through the judicious use of silence and small strategies such as drawing in a distracted class with a quiet, low-pitched, slow, and calm voice? Of course, we understand which person has the most influence in the end. But how often do we apply these principles to our own behavior?

True power does not rely on strength and domination. Strength and domination render us incapable of relating to others and the things around us. The instant we see the world as a set of overt power balances, the instant we have differentiated ourselves from others—whether through imposing our will, competitiveness, or estrangement—we have lost the Way.

We can see how this works on many levels. Say you are being attacked by someone who is trying to hit you. We think we know the right response: hit him back harder than he hits us. But if you understand the Way properly, you do the opposite. You know that the person attacking you will inevitably overextend himself at some point. Your best hope is to try to stay quietly aware of the other person and to guess the precise moment when the over-extension occurs. That is when you make your move and attack, by exploiting your opponent's weakness; the momentum of his overextension is what helps you to prevail over him. This concept is the basis of judo and other martial arts. In Laozi's terminology, you've played weakness against strength.

Anyone trying to dominate you is by definition making distinctions and going against the Way. Weakness, as the *Laozi* uses the term, is on the contrary based upon connecting, sensing, and working disparate elements: this is where its power lies.

> *Those who would take all under Heaven and*
>   *make it theirs, I see that this will be in vain.*
> *All under Heaven is a divine vessel, and it cannot*
>   *be made their own.*
> *Those who make it theirs, destroy it.*
> *Those who grasp it, lose it.*

In the early nineteenth century, Napoleon of France was creating the most powerful army the world had ever seen, and the strongest European empire since the days of Rome. Ambitious and power-hungry, the emperor decided to invade Russia.

Now, the Russian generals had never read the *Laozi*, but they clearly understood the principles behind its vision of power and weakness. When Napoleon invaded their country, they did not try to counter power with power, strength with strength. They *retreated*. When the French armies drove farther into Russia, the Russian armies retreated once more. The French marched deeper and deeper into Russian territory. Slowly the supply lines from their home country became more and more extenuated. The French army made it all the way to the outskirts of Moscow. At this point, the Russian generals retreated again, leaving the city, burning key buildings, and taking with them all of the food. In September 1812, Napoleon captured Moscow and declared himself ruler of the Russian Empire—the greatest imperial figure in all of human history. He sent to the Russian czar, Alexander I, a set of conditions for his surrender. The czar did nothing.

Then winter set in. There was no food in the city, and provisions and other supplies could not be brought through the harsh Russian winter. The greatest army Europe had ever seen began starving to death. Realizing the tragedy that was about to ensue, Napoleon had no choice but to retreat. The weather worsened. By the time the remnants of the army made it back to French territory, a half million men had been reduced to a few thousand. Thus ended the French empire.

> *That which goes against the Way comes to an early end.*

A World That Seems Natural

Let's say you've had a really bad day and feel overwhelmingly stressed out. You didn't sleep well the night before because you had two presentations to prepare for work, and your daughter reminded you at ten o'clock at night that she needed supplies for a school project the next day. You've had one meeting after another all day long, and now it's three o'clock, you've eaten nothing but chocolate, and you have a meeting coming up that you agreed to three weeks ago when you thought you would have time for it. In fact, you had volunteered to *lead* the meeting. You feel irritated just thinking about one more obligation.

So what might happen next? You could rush into the meeting, harried, stressed, angry at your pressure-cooker life, and just get it over with. The others at the meeting would begin to feed off of your stress, anger, and exhaustion. Your feelings would bring out their own stress, anger, and exhaustion. You might start making recommendations, but the others would probably oppose them because of the contentious mood of the room. Minor conflicts would begin to emerge that had little to do with the content of your suggestions. The entire meeting would become an unpleasant scene of conflict, and you would leave feeling even worse than before.

We've all probably sat through meetings like this, where subtle undercurrents of resentment and bad feeling end up undermining things. In fact, most of us have probably had this experience in life in general. It happens when we see ourselves as separate from others and let our unhappiness seep into their experience without our even being aware of it.

The *Laozi* is actually quite specific about who will be most influential in any given situation: it is those who practice nonaction (*wu-wei*), which in the *Laozi* means appearing not to move or act but, in fact, being very, very powerful. Remember the Russian generals who lured Napoleon deeper and deeper into their trap. Those who practice nonaction seem not to act. But in reality, they actually direct everything.

Here's an alternative scenario, one more in tune with the Way. Let's go back to the meeting you had volunteered to lead. It's the same situation: you've had a hard, frenzied day, and this feels like one more obligation on top of so many others.

You rush to the door of the conference room. But this time, before you enter, you stop, breathe deeply, and calm yourself. You are stilling yourself, bringing down your stress levels, and your anger, and getting to that place where you can see everything as undifferentiated. When you still yourself, you're getting closer to the Way.

Then, and only then, after you have gained a sense of stillness, do you walk into the room. You immediately sense the room and all the people sitting there in all of their complexity. You can intuit that there are some people who are stressed, some who are disengaged, and others who are excited to be there. Your job now is to help all these different people reach an accord so the meeting is productive. Without saying a word, with just a glance, you have quietly taken the measure of the people around you.

When you sit down, you don't bellow, "Okay, now listen up: this is what we're going to do!" No, you simply sit down quietly, exuding calm.

Of course, you have an agenda; a set of goals. You know how you want things to go. But instead of stating your position overtly and strongly, you elicit responses from the group. You raise a few questions, bring up a few points, and by the responsive tone you use, the words you choose, and the way you look at people, you create a mood that steers everyone down the path you want them to take. As the other participants begin to talk, the calm, interested, expansive way you respond to them brings out other thoughts. People begin to understand one another well. They begin bouncing ideas off one another, and plans form that you can help shape by encouraging or discouraging through nonverbal communication: smiles, frowns, nods.

Make no mistake: you are in charge. But because of the way you sit and make eye contact with people, the way you express your excitement about their ideas in an engaging tone of voice, your colleagues aren't conscious of the extent to which you are directing the agenda. Slowly a consensus forms, as everyone connects over a certain set of plans.

When the meeting is over, the other participants might go away thinking, *Wow, that meeting went really well; it seemed to run smoothly all by itself*. But in reality, *you* ran the meeting. You shifted the mood of the room completely by your actions—actions that embody the principle of nonaction. Softly, subtly, you created a world in which everyone was connected, excited about their ideas, until what emerged in the end was surely better than what any of them could have come up with before, and yet different from what any of them thought they would want to do when they entered that room. You led by following. And by doing so, you were the Way.

When you become a sage, you don't merely sense people well. Through your softness and suppleness in every encounter, whether with your family, friends, or colleagues, you generate a world around you. You can alter the way other people think and feel by the miniworld you have created.

True influence isn't to be found in overt strength or will. It comes from creating a world that feels so natural that no one questions it. This is how a Laozian sage wields enormous influence.

The Laozian as Leader

When his achievements are completed and tasks
   finished,
The people say that "We are like this naturally."

The enduring power of the *Laozi* lies in its potential to help one become infinitely more influential through softness, not hardness; through connecting, not dominating. But what makes a person so effective in a Laozian sense is the ability to generate a world that feels so natural that we can't imagine it ever having been different, even though it is newly invented. Power and effectiveness, therefore, come not from direct action or overt tactics but from laying the groundwork so that a dramatically different reality comes to be. This is how one can shape things on a small scale, and it can also be how one effects changes that transform the entire world. Let's now take a look at a few historical figures who exemplified this.

In America, we tell our children that our nation is dedicated to the proposition that all men are created equal, as established in the Declaration of Independence.

However, if one looks back to the mid-nineteenth century, this idea was hardly accepted in the United States at all. The founding document of America was then seen to be not the Declaration of Independence, but the US Constitution, which took slavery for granted. In his Gettysburg Address, Abraham Lincoln made the argument that all men are created equal. The president's move was to claim implicitly that the Declaration of Independence was America's founding document, and that we as a nation were dedicated to the proposition that all men are created equal.

When he made this argument, in 1863, it was explosive. The press were incredulous: America was dedicated to no such proposition, nor was the Declaration of Independence the founding document of America. However, Lincoln's vision not only won the day, it also came to be accepted as received wisdom for America as a whole. Today we commonly believe that the Declaration of Independence was the founding document of the United States and that the notion of equality for all was the foundational principle of our nation *from the very beginning*.

This notion would become the basis for many later developments: for instance, a century after Lincoln's speech, Dr. Martin Luther King Jr. argued that when it came to race, Americans were not living up to their own professed values of treating every human being as created equal. He could make this argument only because the notion of equality was accepted as received wisdom. And this notion was only accepted after Lincoln made it so.

And what about the idea of the role of government in American life? We fiercely debate how involved the government should be in order to ensure economic prosperity, but few Americans would assume that the government's role should ever exceed certain parameters.

In the midst of the Great Depression, Franklin D. Roosevelt decided that the United States needed a more expansive government to rebuild the economy and help those in need. When he offered his new reforms, the US Supreme Court argued that such a vision broke from what was allowed in the US Constitution. After many political battles, however, FDR's reforms, which we know as the New Deal, were carried out. Those reforms resulted in the creation of a massive new federal government that regulated the economy, controlled the financial sector, provided financial assistance to the elderly in the form of Social Security, and aided the poor and needy through the welfare system.

To fund these reforms, FDR instituted a more progressive system of taxation than had ever existed before, in which the highest tax rates were in the 90th percentile. This radical new vision for statecraft was so successful that it ultimately became accepted wisdom in America. The model of a regulatory state controlling the financial sector, regulating American commerce, preventing the rise of monopolies, and maintaining a highly progressive taxation system continued for the next several decades. Democrats and Republicans supported it. The only significant tax cut that occurred over the next several decades was established by Democrats John F. Kennedy and Lyndon B. Johnson, who reduced it to the 70th percentile.

This regulatory state built the enormous public infrastructure projects and extensive educational system that helped propel America into the longest period of economic expansion in its history. This model was so successful that other countries looked to the United States as a guide for their own political and economic systems. All of this became accepted wisdom for how to run a state well.

We no longer live in such a world. We cannot imagine anyone in America paying taxes at a rate of 90 percent. We take for granted that a government should play a limited role in regulating the economy and in controlling the financial sector, because we believe these moves dampen economic growth. When did this change occur? In the 1980s.

In 1980 Ronald Reagan was elected president with a radically different vision for America, in which the reforms of the New Deal were portrayed not as having rescued the US economy but as having held it back. Reagan and his fellow Republicans advocated limited government regulation, especially in the areas of the financial sector, education, and public infrastructure, with lower tax rates to stimulate economic development. Although this view was highly controversial when Reagan was first elected, it had become accepted wisdom by the 1990s. Indeed, in the 1990s during the Bill Clinton presidency, this policy came to be known as the Washington Consensus, fully accepted by Democrats and Republicans alike.

Here again, this vision, which became seen as the natural way to run an economy, was exported to the rest of the world as the proper and only way to understand economic and political behavior. Thus, it became impossible to imagine taxing anyone at rates up to 90 percent, even though these were tax rates that once had been seen as completely acceptable and even essential for running a flourishing state.

* * *

So, when did the world we take for granted emerge? How exactly did these changes occur?

In these three cases, Lincoln, FDR, and Reagan were perfectly playing out aspects of the *Laozi*'s philosophy. All three were able to make new and highly controversial positions seem completely natural. In the words of the Laozi:

> *The Way constantly does nothing, yet nothing is*
> *not done.*
> *If lords and kings are able to hold to it, the myriad*
> *things will be transformed of themselves.*

Abraham Lincoln did not argue overtly that the Declaration of Independence was more of a founding document than the Constitution. He did not begin his speech by saying that although the Constitution is the founding document of America, let's just say that the Declaration of Independence is instead. Rather, he wrote one of the most eloquent speeches in the history of America. With his famous opening line, "Four score and seven years ago our fathers brought forth, upon this continent, a new nation, conceived in Liberty, and dedicated to the proposition that all men are created equal," Lincoln rewrote history, alluding to a past that had never existed. Not only was the Declaration of Independence not the founding document, but also the president reinterpreted the statement about all men being equal to include slaves, even though many of the founding fathers (including Thomas Jefferson, who drafted it) were, of course, slave owners who included only white men in their definition of "men." What Lincoln was saying was empirically false on both counts. But by laying out such a compelling and unforgettable vision, he planted the seeds for what would become accepted wisdom. Now we memorize entire passages of the Gettysburg Address, which has become part of the standard rhetoric of the United States in general.

FDR did not present himself as a radical revolutionary, battling entrenched institutions and notions to save Americans in a time of dire need. Instead, he endeared himself slowly to everyday Americans as a congenial grandfather type, who, in his "fireside chats" over the radio, was simply there to help them through the difficult times of the Depression, and to offer a few practical suggestions. Thus, he came across not as a new visionary marking a fundamental turning point in the history of the nation but as a solicitous neighbor offering advice to help people. (He was to use this tactic years later in a move that was to draw an isolationist America inexorably toward war—after having pledged not to enter the raging conflict in Europe—when he gently compared providing arms to our ally Great Britain to lending a neighbor a garden hose.)

Reagan also presented himself as a genial, witty, and kindly figure trying to help Americans return to an earlier, glorious time of individual liberty. Earlier in his political career, as governor of California, he had been a firebrand. As president, however, he drew from softer images that would speak to America's past and present. He created an image of himself as all-American cowboy, referencing his career as an actor and as a commanding leader. He combined that with the mien of a jolly, reasonable paterfamilias. In one televised debate with President Jimmy Carter that was to become the turning point of Reagan's 1980 presidential campaign, he prefaced his response to Carter's points not with direct rebuttal but by simply waving them off, chuckling, "There you go again."

Reagan became the first president to salute the military whenever getting off the presidential helicopter. In the eyes of the public, this move became an iconic image of what a commander in chief does, even though the Constitution requires that the president be a civilian, and military rules dictate that a civilian should never salute the military. But that was beside the point. The salute allowed Reagan to show respect for the military—at a time when the country perceived itself as weak. It soon became unthinkable for an American president not to do so.

Each of these presidents pulled from earlier stock visions of America, such as the great orator calling forth our higher sides or the caring, grandfatherly neighbor. They hinted at traditions, such as Reagan's allusions to the cowboy on the range forging his own glorious destiny. They wove all this into a new vision that eventually ushered in a new reality.

The world we take for granted today is not the world that existed before. All three of these figures were perfect Laozian sages, generating a radically new order that was fully accepted as natural by those within it.

All three were presidents, in positions of authority to begin with. One might assume that gave them a built-in advantage. From a Laozian perspective, though, when you are already in a position of strength, it's all too easy to give in to the temptation to play strength over weakness. But Lincoln, Roosevelt, and Reagan used weakness to effectively generate their worlds—the same approach that worked for Rosa Parks and Gandhi, or that an office worker might use in dealing with a difficult boss. By employing less overt strategies, they were able to accomplish far more than they could have had they tried to impose their wills directly. The argument of the Laozi is that you can always defeat strength through weakness. If you're in a position of strength, play weakness, and if you're in a position of weakness, play weakness. Play weakness regardless of your starting position, and that is how you will shift situations in better directions.

The legend of Laozi as not just a sage but also a god who generated the Way is not as fantastical as it might seem. The Way does not exist in some natural, unchanging order that we must find and harmonize with. Rather, as Laozi shows us, we form the Way by actively weaving together everything around us. Each of us has the potential to become a Laozi—to become a sage—and generate new worlds.

6

On Vitality: The *Inward Training* and Being like a Spirit

Think of the most charismatic, energetic person you know. Have you ever thought of her as someone who is "full of spirit"? Have you ever noticed how being with her picks you up, and fills you and everyone around her with energy?

Or consider how, when you're totally depleted, you say that you're "low energy." Your voice is dull, your mind feels foggy. All you want to do is crawl into bed and take a nap.

We often tend to think that some people are just like your friend: spirited and highly energetic. Or we assume that at the end of a tiring day, it's normal to simply run out of energy—but that we'll regain it with the dawn of a new day.

But how would we live differently if we thought in

terms of being able to become full of spirit through our own training, and were just as aware that we are responsible for our low energy and loss of vitality? The *Inward Training,* an anonymous collection of self-divinization verses from the fourth century BC, focused on this very question. It asked, What does it really mean—and what does it really take—to feel more alive?

To Be like a God

For God doth know that in the day ye eat thereof, then your eyes shall be opened, and ye shall be as gods.

—*The Bible, Genesis 3:5 (King James Version)*

Many of our assumptions about vitality and human agency are based upon age-old notions about divinity. From the earliest days of humanity, people have imitated what they imagined was divine to learn how to live and be a person of consequence.

The most common beliefs about agency are modeled after all-powerful deities and creators, such as the Mohist deity Tian: one who made the world, could move mountains, and had clear standards of right and wrong.

When we think of taking action as standing up for ourselves or getting what we want, and when we think of agency in terms of creating, controlling, or possessing things, we are drawing unwittingly upon the legacy of such notions about divinity. We see ourselves as exercising our own agency along similar, if lesser, lines: we can lift a rock, buy a house, win a race. In these ways, we too effect change and impose our will; wc can even change the very landscape of the earth if we wish.

This is how people have long conceived of agency. Alongside early human impulses to imitate the divine, though, was a growing trend toward cultivating the divine within. The religious movements of the Axial Age rejected old Bronze Age practices of using priests to mediate between humans and the divine, claiming instead that *all* humans possessed some divine potential. In ancient Greece, figures as diverse as Empedocles (a pre-Socratic poet and philosopher) and Plato cultivated these divine aspects within themselves. Plato spoke of "divine ecstasy," and even Aristotle referred to how cultivation could lead to "divine understanding" that transcended the human. Similar movements arose in India: *The Upanishads,* a collection of religious texts, called for people to access the divine directly through cultivation exercises such as breathing and meditation.

Several centuries later, some of the early Christian movements emphasized our ability to uncover our inner divinity. The early Church called these Gnostic movements heretical, insisting on an absolute division between God and humanity; after all, God drove Adam and Eve from paradise for eating an apple that the devil had told them would make them become like God. This injunction—that humans should not strive to become like gods—was powerful precisely because the desire to become godlike had been so persistent throughout human history.

But the Protestant Reformation in the sixteenth century revived the concept of a divine spark within each person, one that provided direct access to God without the mediation of a priestly elite. Human divine potential became even more central in the late nineteenth and twentieth centuries. The nineteenth-century German philosopher Friedrich Wilhelm Nietzsche's assertion that "God is dead" and that man can take his place captured the modern focus on an individual's potential and right to impose his will on the world. Adolf Hitler and Benito Mussolini were to take this one step further: each saw himself as a Nietzschean *Übermensch*, or "superman," creator of a new world order.

Today, even in a far more secular age, there is a resurgence of interest in self-divinization—though we might not name it as such—that is rooted in the earlier Gnostic traditions. We see people around us behaving like gods, whether they are seeking the divine light (or true self) within or acting like masters of the universe. We may debate the extent to which any of us should strive to be this way, and disdain those who seem overly power hungry or narcissistic. But we don't typically question the underlying assumption itself: that we become divine by asserting ourselves. Most of us associate the power rush we feel when living this way with feelings of vitality and aliveness.

This is not the only model of divinity, let alone vitality. The *Inward Training* also called for humans to become more divine. It argued that humans could, and should, alter the world by cultivating themselves to take on divine qualities. But its authors wanted to avoid the emphasis on the will, and so they did not define spirits as figures exercising control over the world or asserting themselves over other people. Instead, they portrayed them as highly refined, charismatic, and attuned beings that transform the world through their sheer connectedness with everything.

This is a different model for human action that can lead us to a different way of thinking about how we should live. When we reconceptualize action and agency as arising from connecting rather than from dominating, we become more divine in an essential way: we become more fully alive.

The Energies of Vitality

We already do lots of ordinary things that make us feel more alive. The simplest of these is taking a deep breath. Though it has now been incorporated into Western medical treatments for anxiety and stress, deep breathing has roots in many ancient traditions. The *Inward Training* teaches that deep breaths are more than simple breaths; we breathe in energy that helps us to soothe ourselves, calm negative emotions, and relax.

Imagine the impact of taking in that sort of energy through these deep, calming breaths all the time, not just during isolated moments in a yoga class or while meditating. We would not become so depleted of energy if we did this on a regular basis.

Or another example: exercise. When you go for a Saturday morning run, you're gathering energy; in fact, you're energizing yourself. Sure, your legs feel like jelly, and you are sweating up a storm. But you probably also feel ecstatic—you feel that "runner's high." What science says comes from a rush of brain chemicals called "endorphins," the *Inward Training* envisions as refined energies or spirit flowing through you. When you feel that highly energized sensation, you see things more vividly, you feel things more keenly, and the walls between you and the rest of the world drop away.

Compare that postexercise exhilaration with the feeling of an exciting creative breakthrough at work. The rush is the same as that when you run: it's a surge of well-being and vital energy coursing through your body. Or think about the feeling of incredible oneness with strangers around you when you are at a music concert or a sporting event. You feel the energy of the crowd pulsating through you; it sweeps you away.

All these energies are the very same thing: energies that heighten your feelings of vitality. Your face is flushed because you feel more alive, not just because you went running. You feel satisfied because you feel more alive, not just because you came up with a great idea for that presentation at work. A deeply fulfilling conversation with a friend doesn't just make you feel more connected; it makes you feel more alive. Whether you're doing something physical, mental, or social, that glowing excitement and oneness with the world are the very same physical feelings. The *Inward Training* says that everything we experience comes from energies called qi and that the most ethereal of these energies—the ones that give us that exhilarated, alive feeling—are the energies of divinity.

What If We Saw the World as Composed of Qi?

As for the essence of all things, it is this that is life.
Below it generates the five grains;
Above it becomes the arrayed stars.
When it floats between Heaven and Earth, we call
* it ghosts and spirits;*
When it is stored within a person's chest, we call
* that person a sage.*

The notion of divine energies was hardly an unusual one in antiquity. In fact, it was a pan-Eurasian concept: in India, there was the notion of *prana,* or "breath," and in Greece there was *pneuma,* or "breath of life," "soul," "spirit." All described a sense that some ineffable, unseen life force coursed throughout the cosmos and was responsible for the origins of life itself.

Today many people would be skeptical that feelings of vitality come from divine energies. But qi is a useful metaphor for what it would take to make us feel more alive, and we can learn from it even without believing it to be true. All we need to do is to think of these energies in an as-if way: What does it mean to act and to live as if we were cultivating qi? And if we do so, how do we live differently? What would our lives be like if we lived as though this framework really exists?

We commonly hold a dualistic worldview: God versus humanity, matter versus energy, mind versus body—we think of these as separate things. But the *Inward Training* holds a monistic worldview, teaching that every single element in the world and in human beings is composed of the same thing: qi. Everything, whether it is mind, body, matter, or spirit, whether it is earth, people, animals, or air, is composed of this very same substance.

But although qi exists in everything, there are infinite gradations of it. Rocks, mud, earth, and other inanimate parts of the cosmos are composed of a low and coarse qi—what we might call turbid qi.

As qi becomes more highly refined, it becomes "vital essence." What sets vital essence apart from all else is that it exists only within things that have life. It is a life-giving force found in plants and animals.

And finally, when qi is at its most ethereal and refined, it becomes divine qi. This sort of qi is so highly energized that it actually affects things around it. This qi is spirit itself. Spirit goes beyond being a life-giving force; it gives living beings consciousness.

A plant has life-giving qi, or vital essence, but it can never be divine; it can never have a spirit. It can never think and process the world. It merely exists in the world. Spirits, though, being divine qi, are fully and vibrantly alive. They have full clarity and see the world with flaw-less consciousness. To be able to see the world so fully is what allows them to act in the world in transformative ways.

And what about us? What sort of energy are we composed of?

We human beings are a combination of the turbid qi of the earth below and the divine qi of the heavens above. We have less-refined qi, including our bodies, but like plants, we are alive, so we also have vital essence. And we even contain within ourselves a little bit of spirit. Unlike plants, we have consciousness, and each of us can effect some changes in the world: we can pick up something and move it through space, throw a ball, open a door. We possess the same potential that the spirits do.

Lessening Our Dependence on External Things

Hold the spirit within, and do not be excessive. Do not allow things to disorder your senses, and do not allow your senses to disorder the mind.

The energy of rocks and plants and spirits remains con-stant. But human beings are different from all other things on earth in that this jumbled combination of en-ergy shifts constantly in us. Over time, we can either be-come more drained of energy and more like the earth, or we can hold on to our spirit and become more spirit-like.

It is difficult to hold on to our spirit. It's more typical

for us to spend our days doing things that drain us of it: We get angry during a fight with our sister over the logistics of a family reunion. We become frustrated by our daily commute and stressed about upcoming deadlines. We feel jealous of a friend, resentful of our spouse, anxious about the future. Every time we find ourselves dominated by negative or extreme emotions, we are allowing external things to sap our energies, allowing these events to wield too much power over us. Every time we go through the daily grind, trudging through our everyday activities, we de-energize ourselves. Our spirit is being drained away, and we are filling ourselves with bad qi instead. This causes us to live so poorly and so out of balance that we get exhausted. We slowly lose our vitality and our sheer embrace of life. If we continue living like this, our spirit will ebb away long before our physical life has ended.

We've already mentioned which types of everyday activities help us to feel more alive. But this doesn't mean that we should start going on more runs whenever we have a spare moment or seeking out our most entertaining friends to keep us feeling exhilarated. Just as external activities and events can make us feel giddy and excited, external events can drag us down. Every day we feel buffeted about by events around us: A lunch with a friend? We feel happy. Someone snubs us at work? We feel depressed. A morning run when the weather feels perfect? We feel ecstatic. We twist our ankle at the end of it? We feel crushed. These emotional extremes are exactly what the *Inward Training* would say devitalize us, exhaust us, and drain us of spirit.

Of course, we all know that sad events trigger negative emotions and drain us. But even exciting and exhilarating events aren't good for us if that's what we depend on to feel a rush of energy.

Triggering events of any sort—whether they make us giddy or jealous or furious—are external. Our emotions are being pulled to and fro by things that happen around us, and any feelings of aliveness we may experience are not steady ones. But these externalities don't have to make us bounce from happiness to sadness and back again. What *is* within our control is the cultivation of balance and alignment, or an inner stability: to be grounded so that we aren't vulnerable to the inevitable happenings of the day.

Cultivating Balance and Alignment

If one is not joyous and not angry, balance and alignment fill the chest.

The *Inward Training* sees the world of our experience as consisting of discrete things that typically interact poorly with one another. This includes human beings and our fragile, imperfect relationships. But the text also describes an underlying Way in which everything is connected. The more these discrete things of the world interact well with one another, resonating with one another, the closer they get to the Way. We get closer to the Way and increase our feelings of vitality when we cultivate the ability to remain balanced. The more stable we are, the more able we are to refine and hold on to good qi.

Like many of our texts, the *Inward Training* moves easily from grand, transcendental ideas to matters that we would consider exceedingly mundane. Concrete, ordinary things are essential means of refining our qi. Since all parts of us—body and mind—are composed of qi, refining the body helps refine the mind, and vice versa. Everything we do to refine one of these spheres will shift our entire being to a more balanced and stable place.

That's why many passages in the *Inward Training* exhort us to pay attention quite literally to our bodies: from standing up straight, with good posture, so that qi can flow unimpaired; to regularly practicing deep breathing, which lets balanced, aligned breathing fill our chests; to eating regularly but in moderation, to keep our qi constant. We might not think that it matters all that much if we stand up straight or sprawl on a couch, or if we are oblivious to our breathing, or if we skip lunch a few days in a row. But what we think of as physical cultivation is responsible for nurturing emotional stability.

At the same time, we should not focus excessively on one area of physical well-being: for instance, becoming obsessed with green smoothies and a vegan diet at the expense of remembering to breathe deeply on a regular basis. We should be aware of maintaining all of these spheres in balance. The alignment this approach brings to our physical body allows us to become receptive to a higher form of qi.

Balancing out different spheres helps to support our emotions as well. Many of us seek tranquility and alignment by withdrawing from the world temporarily, avoiding the various entanglements that draw out all sorts of uncomfortable feelings. So we take coffee breaks, catch a movie, go on vacation or a retreat: this is how we strive to regain balance. But we can experience balance and alignment always—while still fully immersed in the world—by modulating our impulsive desires and being cautious of the ups and downs that come with too much anger or even too much joy.

Many people think of harmony as a onetime action: bringing people who disagree on the best way to tackle a problem into agreement, for example. But the *Wuxing*, another text on cultivation from the fourth century BC, extends the lessons of the *Inward Training* by teaching that it is not only within our means to harmonize discrete, separate elements but also that we must do this constantly.

According to the *Wuxing,* each of us has five potential virtues that need to be cultivated: goodness, propriety, knowledge, ritual, and sagacity. Each one helps us to refine our better sides. But they become problematic if we try to develop one virtue at the expense of the others. There is such a thing as having too much goodness, craving too much propriety, being fixated on ritual, and depending too much on knowledge. If we always relate to other people by exuding goodness, we can easily seem inappropriately gushy in some situations. If we're overly concerned with propriety, we can seem overly formal and distant. If we focus too much on gaining knowledge, we can be too clinical. And concentrating too much on ritual can make us too rule oriented and prevent us from seeing the greater picture.

No one virtue is an absolute norm for how to be. Instead, we cultivate ourselves constantly so that these virtues modulate one another. If we tend to focus too much on behaving appropriately with our coworkers, we can decide to loosen up and make a point of being a bit warmer. If we frequently research new purchases to the hilt, we can temper that tendency by deliberately making our next purchase without reading every consumer review out there. We work on playing our virtues off of one another and recognizing the infinitely interlocking and changing relationship among them, as well as how they give rise to many emotional dispositions. It may seem paradoxical, but we can achieve constancy only by continuously sustaining these moving parts. This is how we get to a more stable place, free from being rocked to and fro emotionally, so that spirit flows unimpeded within us.

Refining Our Response to the World

In classical China, a person who wished to become educated had to first memorize a collection of poetry called the *Book of Songs*. It became part of a learned person's repertoire. People memorized the poems so that, in any situation—the passing of spring, a debate over policy, the joy of new love, the death of a friend—they could quote passages that those around them, knowing the same pieces, would understand.

But the point wasn't to just memorize poems and passively recite them aloud. It was to draw actively upon one's knowledge of the poems and one's reading of the real-life situation and rework them both in innovative ways. By learning to assess situations and then quoting a line of poetry out of context, say, or making a counterintuitive allusion, you would elicit certain emotional responses from you and your listeners, altering their moods and thus moving the situation in a different direction. Poetry became another important means of refining one's response to the world, as people were trained to sense how they could use it to affect listeners for the better.

Music worked much the same way. It was common for music to be both played and performed (like an opera or musical) and to reflect dramatic stories from antiquity. People watched these performances from the time they were children, and the musical repertoire became part of the fabric of their lives. If they found themselves in a situation where they needed to stand up to someone, for instance, they could draw on the emotions they'd felt listening to a piece of music such as the *Wu*, a popular work about a virtuous man who stood up to the arbitrary power of the Shang dynasty to became the first Zhou king. A piece like this informed their sensibilities; it became a part of them.

Music and poetry were important parts of what it meant to become a learned person because they cultivated certain sensibilities of calm:

> To end anger, there is nothing better than poetry;
> To set aside worry, there is nothing better than music.

They cultivated qi by allowing a person to draw on them to feel more responsive, more connected, and more resonant with the entirety of shared human experience. They could induce sudden clarity and moving insight into what it means to be human.

We nourish our qi in similar ways when we marvel over a painting in a museum or feel transported by a piece of music. Anything that inspires awe refines qi by training the senses to respond more profoundly to the world around us. When we are more aware of the world in all its dimensions, we are more open to all that we can potentially feel about it and are better able to react well to it.

Listening to a piece of music that moves us helps refine our experience of human emotion. We are taken through all the life experiences that informed the composer as he created his music; his emotions remain a part of us. We learn what it means to feel those emotions without being pulled to and fro. We can listen to, say, songs from throughout Bob Dylan's career and get the sense of the arc of a life, in both its greatness and pathos. When we find ourselves facing the loss of someone we are close to, a relative's despair, the exhilaration of entering a new chapter in life, we can have a more profound response if we've been listening to music that speaks to us. The music deepens our feeling of connection to our shared humanity.

Poetry and literature work much the same way, allowing us to respond to the world in richer ways. With poetry, certain emotions emerge when we hear words spoken in a certain rhythm and in certain contexts. With literature, we are taken through huge swaths of time or experience from a variety of perspectives that we could never possibly experience in real life. The knowledge we gain provides access to a different way of engaging with the world because it allows us to step outside of our own lives and better empathize with and relate to a vast stream of human experience.

How does this help to refine qi? Music, poetry, art, and literature are composed of discrete elements such as words, notes, sounds, rhythms, and colors. The more we immerse ourselves in them, the more we understand how discrete things resonate with one another, just as qi resonates with qi. They represent how qi relates constantly to all of the other forms of qi around it—for better or for worse.

For most of us, it is worse. Most people interact with one another at an unrefined level; our low-level qi bumps up against other people's qi. When anger or resentment are bound up inside us, when they become our default mode for moving through the day, they tend to elicit similarly negative energies from others. Our worst emotions

THE PATH

play off of other people's worst emotions, setting into motion a negative chain of events.

Imagine what happens if someone nicks your car in a parking lot, and, already stressed by a difficult morning, you lash out at them, causing them to get angry at you in turn for the poor parking job that made it all but impossible for them to avoid hitting your car. The experience will leave both of you feeling furious. But if you have constantly cultivated yourself to refine your qi, this helps you to transform things for the better. You would respond to the parking lot scenario with grace and empathy, the other person would be far more likely to respond with contrition and politeness, and you would both be left with a feeling of goodwill instead of anger. You would be two discrete beings who had tapped into and responded to the best in each other.

Concentrating the Qi As If You Were a Spirit

> *Transforming but not altering qi, altering but not*
>   *changing one's wisdom;*
> *only the superior human holding fast to the One is*
>   *able to do this.*

When you are impervious to the ups and downs around you, when your senses are refined, and your body aligned and healthy, you achieve a settled heart. This is what allows your entire being to become a repository for essence, or spirit:

With a stable mind at your core,
With the eyes and ears acute and clear,
And with the four limbs firm and fixed,
You can thereby make a lodging place for the vital
　　essence.

Qi becomes so refined and concentrated within you that you are like a spirit composed of qi of the highest order; the kind that allows for a life of vitality and longevity. You have learned to *concentrate the qi as if you were a spirit.*

Nietzsche once wrote, "If our senses were fine enough, we would perceive the slumbering cliff as a dancing chaos." We would see to the heart of everything; we would see all clearly. Though he conceived of divinity as a singular being with a will to power, this statement hints at the understanding that spirit can emerge from a different place. There is a different way of being alive and of impacting the world: through your sheer clarity of vision and your connection with everything; with your charisma rather than through your domination.

Charismatic people are not born with transformative abilities; they are born with the *potential* to be so. When that potential is cultivated, the charismatic person becomes capable of drawing others to her through the force of her energy. When we are with someone who is energized in a positive, exciting way—someone who fills a room with her presence and who has a zest for life—we are drawn to her. Her energy is contagious. That charisma comes from spirit. She is charismatic because she is so alive and resonant with those around her. Her refined qi elicits the best of others and draws out their own spirits.

But while the *Inward Training* is almost entirely about cultivation, it is not about *self*-cultivation. A charismatic person is not charismatic because she has a uniquely captivating personality all her own. She is not cultivating herself. She is cultivating energy; she is cultivating qi. She is charismatic and full of life because the highly refined qi within her is identical to the highly refined qi that exists around her. It's by being so resonant with that qi that she becomes able to alter things.

We too can form webs of connection and relationships with people around us by cultivating spirit. People around us can become drawn toward us and enriched by us because of how we energize them. As we become known for being this sort of a person, our relationships and connections grow. We further develop the ability to respond to people at their best. If we encounter someone burning with jealousy or anger, or someone burdened with sadness or anxiety, we become able to respond not to those energies but to the person's other facets, bringing out his or her healthier energies. And as our charisma grows, like a spirit we become able to pull things together, harmonize things, and shift all sorts of situations. The *Inward Training* would say that this highly energized connection with absolutely everything is the Way.

* * *

This is a different notion of agency and of vitality. Divinities are active by resonating with the world, not by imposing their will on it. They don't affect the world by doing the things that we tend to think of as active and powerful, but by seeing things with full clarity, behaving flawlessly without falling into patterned responses, and, through small shifts, resonating with everything around them. What these notions of energies give us is a way to think about moving from a world of endless conflicts among discrete things to a world in which things are ever more harmonious. The more resonant qi we have, the more we can do what the spirits can do, even in our messy, disparate world down here.

Confucius and Mencius elaborated upon how humans can live as fully as possible. The authors of the *Inward Training* tell us that we can divinize ourselves and that is how we live well.

But now comes a philosopher, Zhuangzi, who, rather than trying to divinize humanity, called for transcending the human realm altogether.

7

On Spontaneity: Zhuangzi and a World of Transformation

Zhuangzi dreamed once that he was a butterfly. A joyous butterfly, doing as he chose. He did not even know there was a Zhuangzi. Suddenly, he awoke, and then he seemed to be Zhuangzi. Yet he could not tell if he was Zhuangzi dreaming of being a butterfly, or a butterfly dreaming of being Zhuangzi. Still, there must be a distinction between Zhuangzi and a butterfly. This is called "the transformation of things."

In the famous story of the butterfly, Zhuangzi, a Chinese philosopher from the late fourth century BC, wants to break us from our usual way of seeing the world. We all wear blinders that prevent us from fully experiencing and engaging with the world, and Zhuangzi argues that the greatest of these is our limited human perspective. What if you were not merely a human being but were actually a butterfly dreaming you are a human being? If we could transcend our humanity and know what it means to see the world from all perspectives, we could experience life more fully and spontaneously.

We already know how it feels to experience the world fully and spontaneously. It happens when we experience "flow": the state in which we become so immersed in an activity that we lose ourselves in the joy of what we are doing, whether we are playing soccer, painting a picture, or reading a book. But we tend to think of these moments in the zone as circumscribed ones, reserved for certain activities. We tend to think of flow as something that happens in specific moments when the right conditions align just so.

We tend to not think it's possible to train ourselves to feel that same sort of spontaneous excitement about everything in our lives. But Zhuangzi saw things very differently. He taught that if we could learn to see the world from all perspectives and understand the transformation of things, we would gain a deeper understanding of everything in the cosmos. As we began to break out of the way we typically experience reality, we would learn what it meant to feel spontaneity every moment of our everyday, ordinary lives.

The Way As Endless Flux and Transformation

Like Laozi, Zhuangzi was considered a Daoist philosopher, and the *Zhuangzi*—a text attributed to him and derived from his teachings—a Daoist text. But Zhuangzi would have resisted affiliation with any one school of thought. The only reason that these two very different texts and thinkers have been categorized together is because of their emphasis on the *Dao*, or the Way.

But the Way meant different things for each philosopher. For Zhuangzi, it wasn't about becoming calm and still, or about perceiving the world as absolutely undifferentiated. You could never *become* the Way, just as you could never become the ground from which things grow. Rather, for Zhuangzi, the Way was about embracing absolutely everything in its constant flux and transformation.

The *Zhuangzi* emphasizes repeatedly how everything in the world transforms into everything else in a constant and ceaseless dance of movement and relationships, flux and shifts. Over time everything spontaneously becomes part of something else. This process of change and movement is happening at every moment.

Grass grows, and when it dies, it decomposes, and its qi is channeled into other things. Worms and bugs in the grass are eaten by birds, which in turn are eaten by larger birds or animals. Those larger beasts, too, die over time, decay, become part of the earth, and transform into soil, grass, and other elements. Everything slowly becomes everything else in a cycle of endless change and transformation.

Grass does not plan to become something else when it dies. The transformation just happens. The seasons do not plan to change. The change simply happens.

Birds fly because of their natural endowments: their

wings. They float about depending on the shifting winds and the topography below them. They are spontaneously following the Way.

Fish swim. They too are gifted with natural endowments: gills and tails. They use these to shift and move according to the currents. They, too, are spontaneously following the Way. They don't stop to think, *Now I should turn this way because the current is moving this way, and now I should move that way, because I have to maneuver past that rock*. They just swim.

Zhuangzi referred to the terms *yin* and *yang*, or darkness and light, softness and hardness, weakness and strength. The Way, he argued, is a process of constant interactions between these two elements that seem to stand in opposition but actually complement each other. They must revolve constantly to balance each other. In the winter, *yin*, the cold and dark element, prevails. Then things change, and summer, the season of *yang*, of heat and light, arrives.

The constant and inevitable interplay of the energy of *yin* and *yang* does not just create seasonal change, but also characterizes all the transformations we see throughout the cosmos.

Those Who Do Not Follow the Way

There is just one exception, Zhuangzi argued, to the teeming, transforming world; just one thing in the entire cosmos that does not spontaneously follow the Way. That thing is us: human beings. We alone do not spontaneously follow the Way. In fact, we actually spend our entire lives battling against flux and transformation: we declare our opinions to be right (and others indisputably wrong); we work ourselves up over the accomplishments of a rival; we remain stuck in a dead-end job because we're fearful of change. In the process, we disrupt and block the interplay of *yin* and *yang*. That is due to our own natural endowment: our minds.

What should we do instead? What does it actually mean for a human being to spontaneously follow the Way?

We hear this word *spontaneity*, and we might think we know what that means. After all, we live in a culture that reveres spontaneity. We find predictability boring. We find too many rules stifling. We admire the free thinker, the person who dares to be different, the lone genius who dropped out of college on a whim and founded a start-up. We equate spontaneity with authenticity, increased happiness, and personal fulfillment.

So you might think, *Well, I'm going to just be spontaneous and do whatever I feel like doing.* You could stop what you're doing and dance; you could quit your job, cobble together your savings, and take off on a trip around the world. Isn't that being spontaneous? Actually, no, not for Zhuangzi. Our ideas about spontaneity are almost the opposite of Zhuangzi's. Spontaneity, for him, isn't about doing whatever we want whenever we want.

What we think of as natural spontaneity is the unfettered expression of desires, and there's no way we could embrace that sort of a life all the time. So we go hang gliding, make an impulse buy, or take up a new hobby. We save our spontaneity for the weekends and leave the rest of our lives the same.

True spontaneity requires us to alter how we think and act in the world, to open ourselves up to endless flux and transformation all the time. It requires that we imagine something called *trained* spontaneity—which sounds like an oxymoron but, as we'll learn, really isn't.

Consider one of Zhuangzi's most famous parables: the story of Cook Ding, a butcher. Cook Ding's initial approach to work is to pick up his cleaver and hack away at the meat in front of him. At first, this is just tedious. But over time, the more the butcher does this, the more aware he becomes. He notices that instead of working against all the different muscles and tendons in a chunk of meat, he can find all sorts of flowing channels within each piece. Each is different, and yet they all have lines and joints and paths—places where it is naturally easier to cut. With familiarity and training, he can sense these universal patterns in any piece of meat. He cuts in perfect rhythm, as though he were dancing; the meat falls apart effortlessly before his blade.

But to do this, he can't think too much or approach the task analytically, since each piece of meat is different. According to Zhuangzi, he must value "the Way, which goes beyond technique." He must tap into his divine qualities, those that enable us to resonate well with the world by being connected with it. When the butcher uses his spirit instead of his conscious mind, he senses the Way: only then can he sense the different fluctuations in the meat.

> *A good cook changes his knife annually, since he uses it to cut. A half-decent cook changes it monthly, because he uses it to chop. But there are gaps between the joints, and there is no thickness at all at the edge of the blade. By using what has no thickness and inserting it where there is no gap—there's lots of space to move about in. That's why even though I've been at this for nineteen years, the blade of my knife is as sharp as if it were just sharpened yesterday.*

Cook Ding has understood trained spontaneity.

Note that he did not achieve spontaneity by throwing down his knife and dancing in the streets. He did not cut through slabs of meat on the weekdays but cut loose on the weekends. He achieved spontaneity through the humble activity of cutting the meat over and over until he could just flow with the process. And he was not passive. He flowed with the heavenly pattern of the Way, but he also created something new each time he cut up a slab of meat. By doing so, he found satisfaction and spontaneity in the simple activity that made up his everyday life.

At the end of Zhuangzi's story, a ruler comes to observe Cook Ding at work. "Magnificent," he says. "Having heard the words of a cook, I have learned how to nurture life."

We Already Know How to Become Spontaneous

An experienced cook can whip up elaborate meals without recipes just by using her experience, training, and senses to know exactly how much salt or pepper will bring a dish to life, or exactly how long to simmer a creamy risotto. This is trained spontaneity. A veteran teacher can feel the moment when his classroom is starting to spiral out of control, and quickly grasp what he can do to bring all his students back to a state of calm. His years of experience trained him to respond spontaneously in just the right way at the right moment.

We know that learning any complex skill—be it a foreign language, a musical instrument, riding a bicycle, learning how to swim—requires an initial period of conscious, deliberate training. If you have ever learned to play the piano, you might remember how difficult it was at first, how clumsy your fingers felt on the keys, how confusing it was to associate each with a note, how hard it was to move your fingers independently of one another while your hands glided up and down the keyboard. None of it made much sense at first, nor did it sound very nice. In fact, had you "spontaneously" started pounding away at the keys, it most certainly would have been a painful experience for anyone in the room.

But slowly, over time, you started to get it, to string

together notes that sounded like coherent melodies. Soon you could put left and right hands together, play chords, arpeggios, and tackle more advanced pieces. And that's when the fun really began. You could play pieces from memory and even improvise new ones. Sitting down at the piano became an act of joy as you tapped into excitement and aliveness through playing music. What you were doing once you started to play in this free, spontaneous way was to move with the Way.

Think of how a concert pianist engages with her music and the audience. See the joy that comes from sensing exactly how she should touch the keys to elicit the tones that will resonate between her, her music, and her audience. Through the ability to sense and respond to the world with great skill, the pianist is moving with the Way. Deliberate training is how she arrived at this joyful freedom. It is the same training that enables us to maneuver a car through heavy traffic, lob a tennis ball over the net, or craft a compelling presentation for work. We just "know" what feels right without having to think about it. The effortless competence we develop in all spheres of our lives, from the mundane to the rarified, are examples of trained spontaneity.

The important point is that if we take Zhuangzi's teachings to heart, we are not just becoming skilled tennis players, or employees, or cooks. We are changing our whole approach to life. Our pianist has not trained herself merely to play the piano; she has trained her entire way of being in the world.

Imagination and Creativity

We usually think about training toward mastery as limited to the specific skills we are looking to hone. How could putting in all those hours to master the piano or become proficient at tennis help you to train your entire way of being in the world?

It comes from recognizing the training as not just specific to the skill at hand but as training us to break the limited perspectives that we don't even realize dominate our lives. When we do so, we gain something else too: entry into a state that fosters true imagination and creativity. Although we might not think of being in the zone as related to these things, for Zhuangzi, imagination and creativity stem directly from a state of continuous spontaneous flow.

We often think of creativity as emanating from a single source, a grand Creator. But Zhuangzi would have found such a notion terribly limiting. Instead, he would say that we should think of creativity as emerging when we move beyond the confines of a single great "self" and open ourselves up to the larger cosmos. He would urge us to remember that each of the creatives we revere—a Shakespeare, a Picasso, a Steve Jobs—gained inspiration from opening themselves up to the world, to the Muses, and to boundless curiosity about all that exists. They were opening themselves up to a river of creativity, to what Zhuangzi would contend was the Way.

Trained spontaneity means freeing ourselves of a conscious mind that is by definition restricted to a single self.

Our mind gets in our way, causing us to battle against rather than flow with the Way. Yet in various parts of our lives, we do experience what it feels like to move with it. Think of a get-together with close friends, how the food and the conversation seem to flow effortlessly and joyfully as people become more and more in sync with one another over the course of the evening. You don't have to think to yourself, *Right now I should crack a joke, and in five minutes, I think I'll tell everyone a story about what happened to me during vacation*. The conversation just takes on a life of its own.

Or think of a neighborhood basketball game. You're not using your conscious mind to calculate exactly what you need to do, strategizing that you have to turn 45 degrees this way and stand exactly three feet from the net at this moment. Rather, you flow constantly with a greater sense of your awareness of the whole space, the other players, and all that you must do throughout the game. This greater sense of the whole picture is the source of your prowess.

Even reading the *Zhuangzi* itself allows us to enter an expansive as-if world that opens up our imaginations. Flux and transformation are embodied by the wild and completely improbable stories that fill the text. We hear from fictional creatures; we read stories, like the butterfly story, purporting to tell us what the world looks like through an insect's eyes. We encounter historical figures, such as Confucius, saying distinctly un-Confucian things. There are numerous surprise twists, puns, and poems that defy logic and understanding. The *Zhuangzi* was crafted deliberately to shake up our perspective and make us think differently about reality from the very moment we encounter it.

Of course, we are human; we can't literally become a butterfly and aren't expected to think we should. But by offering this story, Zhuangzi proposes an as-if question: What would it be like if I looked at the world as if I were a butterfly dreaming I am a human being? For that moment, we suspend reality and enter an alternate universe where we expand our ability to imagine all sorts of as-if possibilities in the broadest sense. The entire cosmos is open to us; a world in which everything is flowing into everything else.

None of this is prescriptive. Zhuangzi doesn't tell us what we should do after we gain this different perspective; what comes from that is up to us. The key is the break of perspective itself.

True imagination and creativity don't come from thinking outside the box or letting ourselves go wild, just as true spontaneity does not come from dancing on a table on the weekend while you remain in your tedious job. They don't come out of great disruptive moments that break forth from an otherwise ordinary, drab life. They are part and parcel of how we live our every day; all moments can be creative and spontaneous when we experience the entire world as an open and expansive place. We get there by constantly cultivating our ability to imagine transcending our own experience.

Cultivating Expansiveness

When visiting a museum, we know that if we want to en-rich our experience, we can hire a tour guide, or docent, who can help us experience things through her expert eyes. She can point out recurring motifs or the use of a certain color by an artist, things that we wouldn't have noticed otherwise. We know that if we wish, we can culti-vate expertise in craft beer, or pro soccer, or digital photography—any interest that will enhance our appre-ciation and take our encounters with all of these things to a new level. Our acquired lens adds another layer to our world. We can go into a wine store, for example, and "see" and understand things that we couldn't before; knowing the difference between a cabernet sauvignon and a Syrah becomes something enlivening and exciting. We can un-derstand references to an Arts and Crafts–style house that deepen our reading of the setting in a novel. We don't need to know any of these things to live in the world, but our experience of the world is augmented when we do. We experience the very same reality differently from those who haven't cultivated the same interests. But how often do we think of deliberately applying these principles of cultivation to other, commonplace aspects of our lives so that they can be lived with more expansiveness too?

Charles-Pierre Baudelaire, the nineteenth-century French poet, made famous the concept of a *flâneur*: a per-son who would stroll the city streets observing and taking in, with great openness, all that he saw. If you take a walk with a toddler, or a dog, or your grandmother, you'll notice that they experience the walk differently than you do. The child will stop and gaze raptly at every rock and bug; the dog is tuned into an entire vibrating world of scent; your grandmother might be an avid gardener who names every flower or tree that you see. A walk with someone who has a different perspective on the world can allow you to step outside your normal patterns and to see the world not just differently but also with incredible openness. Through his or her eyes, a casual walk becomes imbued with greater depth and freshness. You read your surroundings differently; new dimensions become visible to you.

We focus on things based on habitual patterns of attention. On our morning commute, we might pay attention to little more than the radio, the exit signs, and the entrance to our parking lot, missing out on other things, such as the majestic sight of a flock of geese heading south. On a walk to the gym a few blocks away, we might be preoccupied by what we want to accomplish during our hour there and not even notice the delicious scents wafting from a restaurant nearby. Our habits limit what we can see, access, sense, and know.

But we all can become more conscious of our tendency to limit ourselves. Seeing the world through someone else's eyes helps us break free and experience even the most seemingly mundane aspects of the world in richer ways. Even a trip to the grocery store becomes more than a tiresome chore if we go with a foodie friend who comes to life thinking of exactly what she could do with all the ingredients she sees. The same store that is so dull for us bursts with aliveness for her because of her excitement about items we wouldn't notice on our own.

That lens is one we can acquire and cultivate. Once we understand how we see the world more expansively when we are with someone who amplifies our own experience, we can develop a nuanced appreciation for the world even when we are alone. We can constantly ask ourselves how someone else would view this world and remain ever aware that our perspective on it is not the only one that exists. As Zhuangzi shows us, it's the principle of seeing things differently, or shifting our perspective, that allows us to experience life with newness and intensity.

Shifting Our Perspective

To wear yourself out to unify everything without understanding that they are the same—this is called "three in the morning." What do I mean by that? A monkey trainer was handing out nuts, saying, "You get three in the morning, and four at night." The monkeys were enraged. So he said, "All right, then, you get four in the morning and three at night." The monkeys were thrilled. There was no difference between name and substance, but their happiness and anger were put into play. He simply shifted with them. This is how the sage harmonizes by using "right" and "wrong"—yet rests on Heaven's wheel. This is called proceeding on two paths.

By now you probably understand how our conscious mind trips us up by clinging to arbitrary, distracting, and useless categories, as shown in the monkey example. There is no overall difference between "three in the morning and four at night" or its opposite, except in how we perceive them.

A radical shift in perspective allows us to view the world in the way that the *Zhuangzi* advocates. This is why it so often turns conventional wisdom on its head: in one story, a grievously disabled man lives his whole life begging for food. He is seen as pathetic, and yet he lives a long time, whereas other young men around him are conscripted into war. So who is the lucky one here?

Our conscious minds tend to focus on what "should be"—on what appears to be right. We think we know what is beautiful, what is large, what is virtuous, what is useful. Yet do we really understand how arbitrary the words and values we depend on actually are?

If a human sleeps in a damp place, his back aches and he becomes stiff. But is this true of a fish? If he resides in a tree, he is fearful and terrified. But is this true of a monkey? Which of these three, then, knows the correct place to live? Humans eat animals, deer eat grass, centipedes enjoy sweets, and hawks like mice. Which of these four knows what food is supposed to taste like? Monkeys mate with monkeys, deer with deer, and fish with fish. People say that Maoqiang and Lady Li are beautiful, but if a fish were to see them it would dart to the abyss, if birds saw them they would fly to the skies, if deer saw them they would gallop away. Which of these four knows what beauty is?

The problem is not simply that we have perspectives. So, after all, do the fish and the birds and the deer. The problem comes when we assume that our perspectives are universal, and we close off our minds. We create rigid distinctions and overly stable categories and values.

But what about categories that do seem clear, and values that seem unshakable and universal? Isn't killing always wrong? How about robbing a bank? Imagine a robber who trains himself to pick locks flawlessly, break into a bank soundlessly, steal money, and escape without detection. If Zhuangzi is denying clear moral categories, then on what basis then could he ever say this is wrong? After all, isn't the robber a perfect example of trained spontaneity?

What Zhuangzi would say, though, is that rigid distinctions lead to such situations in the first place. If you really were training yourself to flow with the Way, you wouldn't be a robber. You wouldn't kill anyone. A robber thinks in terms of distinctions from the start: he thinks in terms of *my stuff, their stuff, I want this, I'll take that.* Someone who kills another is interrupting the flow of the transformation of things by prematurely ending life. For Zhuangzi, the argument against stealing, or killing, wouldn't stem from the fact that they are immoral acts, but that they arise from making rigid distinctions.

Zhuangzi's examples span the entire spectrum from prosaic to grand, but they are all about embracing life. You can embrace life by opening up yourself to see the task of ironing a shirt not as a tiresome chore but as an exercise in cultivating trained spontaneity; a head cold not as inconvenient but as a chance to cozy up in bed reading novels; a canceled wedding engagement not as heartbreak but as an opportunity for a new future. The *Zhuangzi* talks of those who have opened up their perspective fully. By embracing life, they have achieved true resonance with the Way. Metaphorically speaking, they are what Zhuangzi calls "true people." They can "enter water without getting wet and fire without getting burned."

Imagine what it would be like for little things and big things alike to cease to disturb us, instead becoming part of the excitement of life; things we find exciting and embrace. Imagine seeing things from all perspectives, and thus being able to understand that everything that happens is part of the process of flux and transformation. To return to Zhuangzi's metaphor, with this change in perspective, we *would* become true people: able to walk through water without getting wet, through fire without getting burned.

The Final Distinction

If we truly became able to see all things from an unlimited perspective, we could celebrate all aspects of life, including the final distinction: mortality. Death is, after all, only one of the endless cycles of the Way.

Zhuangzi understood the fear of death. He knew that people fear the end of their existence as sentient beings. But in his mind, to think of death this way is to make a false distinction.

Some of the distinctions we perceive are undeniably true. You are you, a human being reading this book, and not the table in front of you or the chair you are sitting on. But these distinctions are momentary. To the extent that you think of yourself in a rigid way—as a human being at a certain moment in time—you risk not seeing yourself as part of a greater world. When you die, that which makes you human becomes part of the larger, natural world. This is nothing to fear:

> *Zhuangzi's wife died and Huizi went to console him. He found Zhuangzi squatting on the floor with his legs open, drumming on a pot and singing. Huizi said, "You lived with her, raised children with her, grew old together. To not cry at her death is bad enough, but drumming on a pot and singing—what could you be thinking?" Zhuangzi said: "Oh, it's not like that. When she first died, how could I not grieve? But then I looked back to her beginning, before her birth. Not just before her birth, but before she had a body. Not just before she had a body, but before she had qi. In the midst of that amorphous*

chaos, there was a change, and she had qi; the qi changed, and she had a body; her body changed, and she was born. Now there is yet another change, and she has died. This is like the change of the four seasons: spring, autumn, winter, summer. Now she is residing in the greatest of chambers. If I were to follow her sobbing and wailing, it would show I understood nothing about our destiny. So I stopped."

Zhuangzi is not saying that death is something to look forward to or to hurry along; on the contrary, life is to be lived to the fullest. Nor is he saying that he did not grieve when his wife died; his grief came, spontaneously. We grieve when people die because we love them and miss them.

Indeed, if we think of death purely from a human perspective, it is profoundly terrifying: it is annihilation of that part of us, or a loved one, that is human. But when we view death from the broadest possible perspective, we feel grief but also see, as Zhuangzi did, that our human form is a wonderful but temporary moment among all the transformations that make up the Way. We understand that this person has always been part of the Way and is still part of the Way. That person will become part of the grass, part of the trees, a bird soaring in the sky. If we understand that the stuff that is us has always been a part of the flux and transformation of the cosmos and always will be, then we no longer need to fear death; we become free to fully embrace life. We do away with the last of the distinctions that limit our experience of the world.

Through all the parables and anecdotes in the *Zhuangzi*, we are meant to consider what it would be like to be liberated from our confining, singular human perspective. On a metaphorical level, this means seeing the world as a butterfly, a bird, a tiger. On a more immediate level, this means understanding the world from another person's point of view. If you're a woman, imagine seeing the world as a man. Or seeing the world from an old man's perspective, even though you're young. Or putting yourself in the tattered shoes of an impoverished artist, despite your being a wealthy lawyer. Imagine seeing the world through the eyes of an ally—or an adversary. Opening up to the possibilities of all perspectives allows us to see the entire cosmos from the most expansive place possible, which is how we begin to understand the endless transformation of things.

This is the vision Zhuangzi proposes: unlimited perspective and trained spontaneity. Our ability to transcend the human comes precisely from the fact that we are human. We can embrace far more of the cosmos than any other creature on Earth because of our vast capacity for imagination. Only we can enter endless as-if worlds to see the universe through the perspective of another. We get there only through the constant work of keeping ourselves open to everything, moving spontaneously with the Way, and becoming an active part of the transformation of things.

8

On Humanity: Xunzi and Putting Pattern on the World

We often hear that self-acceptance is the key to personal growth: *Love who you are. Be at peace with the person you are in this moment.* This leads us to accept not just ourselves but also our lives; in doing so, we gain some measure of serenity.

But one of our philosophers would have been concerned about this level of self-acceptance. Xunzi, a Confucian scholar born in 310 BC, didn't believe we should accept ourselves as we are. Rather, he argued that we should never complacently accept what we think is natural to us.

Yes, just about anyone would rush to rescue a child from a well, but Xunzi didn't want us to forget our less altruistic impulses in everyday moments. Our very worst cravings and desires are also a part of what's natural about us.

We feel a flash of rage when stuck in traffic and someone beeps at us to get moving. We gossip about a friend's misfortunes, spilling secrets she's shared in confidence. We stew for days over a critical remark someone made to us; we binge shop online to quell our anxieties. Imagine what it would be like if we always allowed our worst, undomesticated sides to emerge constantly—if we accepted our "authentic" selves in every moment. As Xunzi wrote:

> *Human nature is bad. Its goodness comes from artifice. It is in the nature of humans to be born with a fondness for profit . . . They are born with hates and dislikes . . . That is why people will inevitably fall into conflict and struggle if they simply follow along with their nature and their dispositions.*

For Xunzi, the notion that "natural is better" was dangerous. And he wasn't referring just to human nature. He was also referring to our assumption about the world at large.

Patterning the World

Consider the following tale, a story much like the many as-if stories that Xunzi told:

> *In distant antiquity, at times the rains would come, at times they would not. No one knew when. At times it would be cold, at times it would be hot. When it was cold, humans, who had no clothes to*

wear, were at risk of freezing to death. When rain did not fall, plants did not grow. When the rains came, plants and berries grew, which humans could eat to nourish themselves, but just as often the plants were poison, and made them ill.

Gradually humans began to understand that these events were not random. They came to realize when it would rain and when it would not; when it would be cold and when it would be warm. They began to realize which plants they could eat, and which were poison. They began to domesticate the plants. They would plant them according to the changes in the weather, which they came to know as the seasons. The process continued as they cleared more ground for planting, domesticated animals to help with the process, and drove out those animals that they could not tame.

Eventually, what had once seemed like unpredictable chaos of natural phenomena—random rains, wind, cold, heat, nourishment, and poison—were turned into a harmonious system. That which grew from the earth was now correlated with the larger patterns of the heavens. But this was not natural. Humans had domesticated the world. Humans had made it so that these disparate phenomena became a harmonious set of processes.

This story about the invention of agriculture reminds us that the world as we know it was constructed by humans, who took elements in nature and reconstituted them, reworked them, and domesticated them to serve human needs.

In other words, human beings are the ones who give pattern to the world. Xunzi reminds us that we were born into this world, but the patterns we see in it were created by us:

> Heaven and Earth gave birth to us. We give pattern to Heaven and Earth. We form a triad with Heaven and Earth, are the summation of the myriad things, and are the father and mother of the people. Without us, Heaven and Earth have no pattern.

He thought that any loyalty to nature, whether it is our own human nature or the nature out there, any acceptance of the world "as it is," was inherently limiting and destructive. He asks us to consider how we would live differently if we understood just how much the world is already our creation. If we have made the world that we experience, then we should not be asking ourselves how to find our proper place within it. We should be asking whether we have structured it well.

The Age of Xunzi

Xunzi, who lived about two hundred fifty years after Confucius, is a fitting cap to our exploration of Chinese philosophy because of how he synthesized the works of all the thinkers who came before him.

A highly respected teacher and the leading Confucian scholar of the day, Xunzi lived at the end of the Warring States period, the events of which very much shaped his thought. By this time, several states had become highly militarized and dominant, and it was clear that whichever one took power would bring about a world in which the ideas of Mencius would be inadequate.

The new political climate influenced the intellectual world. Witnessing the disorder and chaos of the times, thinkers such as Xunzi sought not just a unifying solution to the political situation, but also a synthesis that would take the disparate lines of philosophical thought from past eras and unify them into a coherent whole. Just as he portrayed humans as actively weaving together random natural elements to pattern the world, he gave pattern to the many vibrant ideas and notions of the past three centuries.

As Xunzi developed his philosophy, he came to believe that the thinkers preceding him had indeed captured concepts of great significance. Mencius was right to focus on self-cultivation, for example, and the Laozian idea about how we connect things was crucial. But he also argued that each of these thinkers had blind spots. Each had understood something important, but none saw the big picture.

None but Confucius, that is. Xunzi believed that Confucius alone had understood the most important, most fundamental practice: that of ritual training to become a better person.

But Xunzi would do something very different with

ritual. For Confucius, ritual was a means to construct miniature as-if moments endlessly to create pockets of order in human relationships. Xunzi expanded this notion so that instead of constructing pockets of as-if moments, we could create vast as-if worlds. He believed that ritual works to transform our natures when, and only when, we recognize it as the artifice it is. It is that very consciousness of artifice that Xunzi exhorts us to apply to the world at large. This is how ritual not only helps us to become better people, but to construct a better world.

The Importance of Artifice

In his writings, Xunzi famously likened human nature to a crooked piece of wood, one that had to be straightened forcibly from the outside. But unlike other commentators on human nature (such as Kant, who centuries later would declare, "Out of the crooked timber of humanity, no straight thing was ever made"), Xunzi believed that the crooked wood of human nature *could* be straightened. It just required *wei,* or "artifice," from which ritual emerged.

But that artifice had to be used well. We tend to distrust those who seem artificial or phony. However, as Xunzi would likely remind us, each of our personas is constructed. Even when we think we're being natural and "real," being like that is a choice, and thus it is a kind of artifice too. For Xunzi, being artificial is a good thing—as long as we're aware we are doing it so that we can do it well.

Artifice helps us corral our spontaneous natures and unruly emotions. A toddler throws a noisy tantrum when he is tired, hungry, and doesn't get to play immediately with his favorite toy. But as adults, we are capable of more self-control. When we haven't slept well, are famished, and are all packed up and about to leave work for the day, if our coworker asks for ten minutes of our time to discuss a problem she is having with the boss, we don't submit to what we "naturally" feel and throw our coffee mug at her head in annoyance and tell her absolutely not. We act as-if. We tell her that of course we have time for her, it is our pleasure—and, as we help her, we find ourselves enjoying the interaction, we feel better for having taken the time to assist a colleague, and we forget that we are tired and hungry. When we end up leaving for the day fifteen minutes later than we'd planned, we are in better spirits than we would have been had we succumbed to who we "naturally" and really are.

That which is used as it was from birth is called human nature. The part of human nature that . . . resonates and responds spontaneously and without interference is also called human nature. The likes, dislikes, happiness, anger, sorrows, and joys of human nature are called emotions.

When the emotions are thus, and the mind acts [wei] upon them and makes choices, this is called thinking. When the mind thinks and is able to act [wei] upon its thoughts and move, this is called artifice.

169

Xunzi argued that we should consciously work on our natures to help us refine and order our emotions and impulses. Through artificial constructs such as rituals, we can impose patterns on our natures much as agriculture gave pattern to the world around us. We can control our impulse to have a tantrum like a toddler, and in doing so, we are helping to shape our responses to things.

But there is a paradox: if the sages were human, with inherently bad human natures, how did they come up with the idea of creating rituals in the first place? How could they transcend that stew of questionable human impulses to consciously act better?

In another as-if story, Xunzi asks us to imagine how the sages came up with these innovations that would help us to live well together. He compares this innovation to making pots:

> All rituals and propriety were generated from the artifice of the sages. Thus a potter kneads clay and makes vessels; the vessels are generated from the potter's artifice, not originally generated from human nature . . . The sages accumulated their considerations and thoughts and made a practice of artifice and precedents; they thereby generated rituals and propriety and made laws and standards arise.

One might assume that Xunzi was comparing the creation of human standards, laws, and rituals to the creation of pottery: two grand ideas that transformed what humans can do. But on the contrary, he was actually comparing the creation of human society to the humdrum, incremental work of learning over time how to make *a* pot. He was calling attention to the idea that ritual didn't merely emerge by happenstance; it was an intentional, created endeavor. The creation of ritual by the sages was like the actual work a potter does to train herself to make a pot, by working with and feeling the clay, and imagining what shape it should take. The sages applied artifice to their human natures and honed their senses to perceive how people's interactions might be shifted and to imagine what sort of as-if interactions could help them to live well together. Over time they were able to produce rituals precisely as a potter learns how to produce a pot. In Xunzi's mind, the rise of human culture and social rituals came not as one great innovation but through everyday craft, generated through artifice.

Human nature is the basis, beginning, material, and substance; artifice is the pattern, the principle, and the source of abundance and profusion. If there were no human nature, there would be nothing for artifice to add to. But if there were no artifice, human nature would be unable to beautify itself . . . When human nature and artifice combine, all under Heaven is put in order.

Our nature, given by Heaven, awaits the patterning of human activity. The result is a thing of beauty: humanity elevated to an unimaginable degree.

The Danger of Thinking the World Should Be Natural

If you use a chariot and horses, your feet have not improved one bit, but you can travel a thousand li. If you use a boat and paddle, you haven't learned to swim, but you can still cross the rivers and seas. One who is cultivated is no different from others at birth; he is simply good at making use of things.

Many people worry about the impact of human "progress" on our globe and climate. We debate the ethics of genetically engineered crops or stem cell research, fret over toxins in plastic wrap or the use of fluoridated water. We see kids glued to electronics and wonder what happened to the days when childhood was spent playing out in the backyard. Many of us respond to the onslaught of technological advances by romanticizing the natural, wishing we could go back to a time before human actions seemed to make everything worse. And these are understandable concerns in this hyperconnected, hyperengineered era. But is natural always better?

Not surprisingly, Xunzi didn't think so. In his time too, there were longings for a more natural world. But Xunzi had much to say about the dangers of blindly revering nature.

Xunzi saw our ability to create an artificial, constructed world as a good thing. After all, the world in its natural state is full of struggle. Fish swim and birds fly, and it is true that these actions flow with the Way, but those fish include salmon, battling their way upstream to return to their birthplaces to spawn. Those birds include birds of prey, swooping down fiercely on small, frightened animals. All these creatures are living spontaneously in accordance with nature. And we, too, left in our natural state, would spontaneously live this way. But we shouldn't want to be like nature, endlessly spontaneous and endlessly struggling. We, uniquely among all these living creatures, can construct worlds within which we can transform ourselves and transcend this natural state. The mind's tendency to distinguish us from the rest of the world is an asset, one that allowed us to create human morality, rituals, and innovations.

The danger of thinking the world should be natural is that it prevents us from recognizing what great things we are capable of creating, and it negates our responsibility for the world around us. Xunzi wanted us to harness the mind to improve upon our natural selves and our natural world and become the best human beings we can be.

Remember Zhuangzi's story of Cook Ding, who eventually became so able to sense the patterns in the meat that his knife flowed between them and never needed to be put to the grindstone? While Zhuangzi would see these patterns as existing in nature, Xunzi would challenge the notion that anything about this scenario is even natural at all. He would have us remember that the ox that the meat comes from is domesticated; the knife is manmade. The very fact that Cook Ding has a job as a butcher is an artifice; the job was created by humans. The entire situation is a social construction. The patterns that emerge are the result of human interventions, and that is where our focus should be. We domesticate, organize, and pattern nature. How we do so is up to us.

Nothing Is Natural

In Xunzi's tales of the invention of human civilization, he reminded us that human endeavors were about building on what is "natural" and making it incomparably better.

By putting pattern on the world, we left behind an era in which humans would freeze to death in the winter because they had no clothing, had to live in caves and in trees because they had no shelter, and had to forage for food, occasionally finding edible berries but just as likely dying from poison berries nearby. With the innovations of clothing, shelter, and agriculture, we domesticated the natural world and transformed it for our own prosperity.

Of course, human intervention can also have many dangerous ramifications. Xunzi's response, though, would not be to pull back from intervention but to encourage us to become conscious that we have created the world we live in and notice where we have made mistakes, so that we can improve upon them, intervene better, innovate better, create better.

We have already imposed "pattern and order" on our world. Some of these constructions are apparent to us; others, less so.

Here's one example: we often use the word *natural* in relation to childbirth. Usually proponents say that a natural childbirth is childbirth the way nature intended it: no medications, no interventions, sometimes even outside a hospital. This is said to be the way that women used to give birth before the advent of medical interventions. The implication is that natural is better for both mother and child.

But actually, what we think of as natural childbirth in the modern age is itself filled with interventions. One of the most revolutionary of these is hand washing by the birth attendant. The maternal mortality rate in the period immediately following birth used to be very high; one of the leading causes was postpartum fever from unsanitary conditions. When a Hungarian doctor named Ignaz Semmelweis noticed in the mid–eighteen hundreds that women giving birth in hospitals had a much higher rate of mortality than those who birthed at home, where there were fewer foreign germs for the body to contend with, he embarked on a large-scale study to investigate the cause. He was ridiculed for his conclusion that hand washing with an antiseptic could drastically reduce these deaths. (One doctor responded, "Doctors are gentlemen, and gentlemen's hands are always clean.") While the hospital where Semmelweis worked took up his suggestions and reduced its maternal mortality rate by 90 percent, his recommendations were largely ignored elsewhere. Semmelweis, broken down by the criticism and lack of faith in his idea, died in an asylum at the age of forty-seven. It wasn't until the French microbiologist Louis Pasteur proved the existence of germs several decades later that doctors began washing their hands as a matter of routine before attending a birth.

Today hand washing is considered a necessary precaution and perfectly natural, but it was a human discovery that took decades to take hold. And Xunzi would have us remember the need for it was the result of the innovation of hospital birth, itself a response to changes such as the rise in population, but also the cause of a new danger: exposure to foreign germs. Any innovation gives rise to new problems that then need to be solved. But Xunzi would not say that the solution is to return to a time before the innovation. He would remind us that we can build on innovations, creating further advances to address the problems created by the previous one.

Here's another one: we fear the increasing prevalence of genetically modified crops, and even require that genetically modified foods be labeled. Such genetic modifications raise fears of humans playing God and manipulating the natural order. In fact, most of the foods we consume today have been modified over the past several millennia. Without going deep into the forests to forage for, say, mushrooms or wild berries, you would be hard pressed to find food that is not the product of some sort of human domestication. The current mode of genetic modification simply allows us to alter plants more quickly than we have been able to do up until now.

Of course, not all genetically modified foods are being modified in a good way. However, Xunzi would say we should not assess our food in terms of how "natural" it is. The real question should be: in each instance, are we employing artifice wisely and well?

Our longing for a natural world arises in discussions of the Amazonian rain forest. We are alarmed—with good reason—at the current destruction. But those concerns are often voiced as despair that we are destroying one of the last remaining natural parts of the Earth. In fact, archeological work has demonstrated conclusively that much of the Amazonian rain forest is itself a product of domestication by indigenous peoples. Preserving the rain forest as it is would not return it to a natural state; it would preserve a different type of human domestication. The debates over conservation of the rain forest are significant and have far-reaching implications, and they would be more productive if we took the question of what is "natural" off the table.

We've created the world we live in, and we can choose to move it in a different direction. Subjects such as the best way to preserve the Amazon, or whether or not to pursue cloning or genetically modified foods, are difficult to discuss wisely when they devolve into debates about what is natural versus artificial. These misguided debates prevent us from facing up to the real issues at hand. If we fetishize nature, we surrender our human power to transform the world, and fail to acknowledge that just as we have created problems in the world, just as often we have improved upon what exists in nature.

If we do not see the positive aspects of human manipulation of the world, we tie our own hands and blind ourselves to the subtleties of issues such as environmental protection and stem cell research. We should simply ask: Are we doing these things well or not? If not, what improvements can we make?

Just as there are those who romanticize the natural, there are also those who revere technology and think newer and bigger are always better. But just as nature is not something to blindly accept, neither is artifice. It is true that technological advances have led to many new inventions that make life easier. But Xunzi would say that both camps—those who romanticize technology and those who demonize it—misunderstand how we should approach artifice. Endless technological innovation isn't what matters; it's what we do with it and how we build on it in each particular situation.

We have created an artificial, constructed world, one with immeasurably grave problems. But that does not mean that we should surrender our human power to transform it for the better. Instead, by understanding what we have done, we can change where we go from here.

Constructing a World

Water and fire have qi, but they do not have life. Grass and trees have life, but they do not have understanding. Birds and the beasts have understanding, but they do not have propriety. Humans have qi, life, and understanding, but they also have propriety. Thus, they are the most precious thing under Heaven.

Xunzi believed that we alone, out of all the creatures in the cosmos, are capable of vastly exceeding our capabilities and making good lives for ourselves.

In saying so, he was building on the concepts of thinkers who came before him. But his ideas also very much reflected the turbulent age in which he lived, in which powerful states had created huge bureaucratic institutions and were gathering unprecedented momentum in their campaigns to found a new dynasty that would unify China.

Many voices called for reducing these states' power and for returning to a more virtuous age. But for Xunzi, it was clear there would be no returning to the past and that the shape of the dynasty to come would be very different from what had come before. For him, the way forward did not lie in rejecting these powerful state institutions, despite their troubling aspects. Rather, people needed to work with what they had. They needed to learn to use these new institutions well; to reframe what already existed in order to build a state that would enable social mobility, and to create a world in which the educated elite ruled. Building such a meritocracy would be, for Xunzi, how humans could most wisely give pattern to the world.

In giving philosophical pattern to the world, Xunzi took stock of the vibrant ideas already out there. He agreed with Laozi's concept of generating worlds, but he found dangerous the notion of generating a world that appears natural but isn't so. Think of a cult leader who lulls his followers into believing in his catastrophic vision; think of Hitler, who slowly generated a natural-seeming world that ended in inhumane devastation.

Xunzi understood the *Inward Training*'s call for cultivation. But cultivating our divinity in order to resonate with the world around us can easily lead us to transcend our humanity, the very thing that he argued endows us with the ability to create a better world. We shouldn't aspire to be like a resonant spirit. We should be working on the messy, human stuff that is us.

At a broad historical level, Xunzi wove together the thought of the previous two centuries. In our own lives we can do the same. We can consider what it means to behave in a more Laozian fashion in some contexts, or in a more Zhuangzian or Confucian way in others. Like Xunzi, we too can see how all the thinkers were onto something important, while recognizing the limitations and weaknesses of each of their ideas.

We are always creating ourselves, always creating the world; we, and the world we live in, are already products of artifice. It is self-cultivation alone that enables us to exceed what we thought we were while remaining fully human. Once we understand what it means to create wisely, we can remain open to all the possibilities that lie before us. Once we recognize how we've already shaped our surroundings, we can take on our role as the only beings in the cosmos who can give pattern and order to the world. Nature out there is the same as nature within: it's something to be worked on, altered, and made much better. We've constructed this world; therefore, we can change it.

9

The Age of Possibility

Confucius said, "At age fifteen I set my intention upon studying; at thirty I established myself in society; at forty I freed myself of delusions; at fifty I understood the mandates of Heaven; at sixty I could hear with clarity; and at age seventy what my heart desired and what was right came into alignment."

We began this book with some strong claims. We proposed that all of us have assumptions about who we are, how our society operates, and our place in world history. And we argued that many of these assumptions are flat-out wrong—not only empirically wrong but also dangerously wrong, for if we live according to these assumptions, we limit our experience and our potential dramatically.

One narrative has taken over all others: that we have broken from the repressive past of a traditional world and now live in a modern one in which we are free to live our lives. This master narrative has been so pervasive and powerful that, over time, we have come to accept it as utterly true and natural. It has directed our assumptions and our actions without our even realizing it.

Per our definition, a traditional society is one in which a stable self and a fixed, coherent world are assumed; in which one flourishes by following larger societal norms unquestioningly; in which there is minimal social mobility; and in which one lives within a confined worldview closed off from other ideas.

But if this is how we do indeed define the traditional, then *we* are the ones who are accepting a traditional worldview and returning to a traditional society. Whether it is at a personal level (the way we confine ourselves in our interactions, the way we limit decisions about our future) or the societal (the aggregation of wealth in the hands of an elite few, greatly decreased social mobility), in both realms we are steadily slipping back into a traditional world.

Our notions of tradition and modernity have led us to see everything on a spectrum, with the traditional world at one end and the modern world at the other. But there is a completely different axis from which to view things, in which the stable/authentic/sincere stands in stark opposition to the broken/fragmented/messy world as seen by our philosophers.

The Chinese philosophy we have explored in these pages can break us from the confines of our narrative, as well as from the assumptions we hold about who we are and what kind of world we live in. Far from seeing coherence, sincerity, and authenticity as modern, we can recognize how these ideals have shackled us. Working through complexity and fragmentation is how we can break from where we are. It is by opening ourselves up to fresh—if challenging—notions that we will leave the traditional world and truly become cosmopolitan.

How We Became Traditional

Why were these ideas lost to us in the first place?

We learned about the Axial Age, a period during which religious and political experimentation flourished throughout the continent of Eurasia following a radical break from an aristocratic past. But then the religious and political experiments ended, at least in some parts of Eurasia.

In the western portion of Eurasia, when the Roman Empire fell, Europe reverted to rule by aristocratic lineages. Again it became what people would look back upon centuries later as a traditional world—one in which social positions and political power were determined solely by birth. This was the hereditary social world that would eventually be overturned in the nineteenth century.

This world was politically fragmented. Aristocrats controlled their own regional domains. The rulers of each domain made their own customs and decrees as they wished, with no coordination or consistency among them. With no overarching state to create comprehensive laws, no roads or other public infrastructure were built to connect these territories. Not only was there no social mobility, but also the lack of transportation routes made it impossible for any mercantile activity to develop.

It was not until over a millennium later that the beginnings of what we think of as the modern period began: the emergence of Protestantism and its emphasis on the individual, the emergence of urban areas and a market economy, and eventually a middle class that would begin calling for political power of its own.

* * *

Everything we've mentioned had a profound impact on both the development of Europe and the way we have come to think of China.

In Europe, the break from an older, hierarchical world structured by birthright was temporary, and it quickly reversed back to the aristocratic mode when the Roman Empire fell. But in some other parts of the world, that break from the traditional past was more enduring.

During the age of the early empires, China's first significant empire, the Han, formed effective states and used bureaucracy and law to undercut hereditary rule. Even after the Han dynasty fell in the third century, subsequent empires would continue pushing for the creation of successful state bureaucracies that allowed China to flourish.

In the early seventh century, for example, while northwestern Europe was still dominated by small, feudal enclaves, a vast new empire emerged in China: the Tang. Run by an effective bureaucracy and legal system, the Tang created a thriving, vibrant, and cosmopolitan society, its capital filled with peoples, goods, and religions from all over Eurasia.

By the twelfth and thirteenth centuries, these great governing bureaucracies in China had become truly meritocratic institutions: every single position of power, except for the emperorship, could be gained only by becoming educated and taking the civil service exam.

The exam was not aimed at gauging what inborn talents a candidate possessed or what skills and abilities he could demonstrate. Rather, during the exam, a candidate would be asked questions about real-life scenarios that any official would likely face: situations full of moral quandaries and conflicting, incompatible interests. He was not judged on the right answer, because there wasn't one. He was evaluated on the promise he showed to see the whole picture and navigate complex moral situations. The exam was a measure of goodness.

Of course, this system wasn't totally accessible to all. To begin with, the exam was restricted to males. And just as elsewhere in the world at the time, there was no universal education. Wealthier families could arrange for their children to be tutored for the exam. But a student preparing for the exam was being educated in moral self-cultivation and learning a different set of values than those of the aristocratic elite. When he took the exam, his answers were anonymous; it didn't matter who his family was. And if he passed, he would be transferred from place to place, far from his home region, so that his judgment would not be overly influenced by childhood connections or powerful local interests.

What this meant was that political power was not hereditary. It was held by an educated elite.

Freed of the vested interests of the aristocratic elite, the state could focus its energy on public infrastructure projects in a way that was not possible in the decentralized, disconnected world of feudal Europe. In China, roads were built, canals dug, extensive legal systems developed. All this was highly productive for the growth of the economy. And as the economy took off, huge trade networks began developing across China and extending well beyond its borders. These networks played a major part in the trade systems that started spreading through Southeast Asia, across the Indian Ocean, and into the Middle East in the fifteenth through eighteenth centuries. The trade networks also ultimately connected China and the Mediterranean region. Venice, for example, became incredibly wealthy largely from selling and buying goods along these networks.

While this enormous maritime economy was beginning to transform much of Eurasia, parts of Europe continued to be "traditional," still run by aristocratic clans. Northwestern European countries such as the Netherlands, Spain, and England—far removed from these trade networks and from the wealth they were creating—began building ships to sail around the southern tip of Africa and on to Asia, and then later to sail westward around the globe. Instead of reaching Asia, however, they landed in the Americas. They began to build a new colonial economy across the Atlantic Ocean based upon slave labor.

This new colonial economy began bringing wealth to western Eurasia. But wealth alone did not create states. And that is the next part of the story.

* * *

As early as the sixteenth century, Jesuits started traveling to China. They were stunned by what they saw. And they began writing accounts to describe it: bureaucracies run by an educated elite, not aristocrats; laws applying to all, whether peasant or aristocrat; people who became educated in order to take a civil service exam; social mobility through a meritocracy. All this was simply unheard of in Europe.

Two centuries later, these accounts helped to spawn an entire movement in Europe called the Enlightenment. Philosophers such as the French writer Voltaire (1694–1778) read these accounts and asked how they could replicate what they described. They began to develop ideas for institutions that could foster bureaucracies, laws, and an educated elite. European rulers realized that having such institutions was entirely possible. After all, they existed in China.

They started building effective states, establishing legal systems, and creating strong militaries. With the wealth coming in from the Atlantic economy, these new states became tremendously powerful and were finally in a position to connect to the Asian trade networks. But now the goal was not just to reach those networks; it was to take them over, as they had the Americas—to colonize them and create an empire.

This is when the intriguing twist on how we look back at history began to occur. When these European states became wealthier and stronger and began to break down the older aristocratic orders, they saw themselves as creating a rupture in history: rejecting the traditional world and beginning a modern one. Thus, they thought the Asian territories they were colonizing to be backward and traditional. Now they could be liberated—by becoming more like the West.

Generations of Western thinkers perpetuated this view of China as stuck in an earlier stage of evolutionary progress. The German philosopher Georg Wilhelm Friedrich Hegel (1770–1831) described the Chinese as rooted in a state of perpetual harmony with nature. He believed that progress was possible only when states had reached the stage he saw Europe at: rational, self-aware, broken free of the natural world, and able to consciously engage in struggle and conflict that would help continue their progress. The sociologist and economist Max Weber (1864–1920), also from Germany, tried to understand why capitalism had never emerged in China the way it had in Europe. He concluded that China's lacking a set of transcendental principles had limited it. He argued that Confucianism and Protestantism had laid very different philosophical foundations that led China to adapt to the world, while the West sought to transform it.

Yet there was no doubt that much of what Europe inherited—and, by default, our twenty-first-century world, too—has its roots in China. The general concept of meritocratic exams (such as the Scholastic Aptitude Test, or SAT, the standardized test used for admissions at US colleges) can be traced ultimately to China. Laws that apply to everyone equally originated in China, as did bureaucracies run by an educated elite.

And there is a little caveat to the story of what Europe learned from China. Only one facet of these ideas made it: the ideas of Mozi and his intellectual descendants, the Legalists. The ideas that spread throughout Europe portrayed human beings as rational agents running rational legal systems based upon universal laws. Their exams measured pure ability, not moral goodness or moral training. These Mohist ideas were taken out of the moral framework in which they had been embedded and were seen purely as a vision for how to create a bureaucratic government. Legalism became a key ingredient in the rise of what we think of as the modern, rational state. The ideas that Westerners left behind were those having to do with moral training, goodness, and self-cultivation.

So while forms of statecraft from Asia were imitated, they were employed differently. In China, the goal had been to divorce wealth from political power so that the state could function as a meritocracy run by an educated elite. In the West, though, the strategy was to break down

aristocratic societies by trying to connect wealth and political power as much as possible. Social mobility would
be established through acquiring wealth—which would
then lead to direct access to political power. The driving
force behind social mobility in the West would not be
education, but wealth. Not the state, but the economy.

This is one way to break down an aristocratic world.
But it is not the only way. And by thinking of all of previous human history as "traditional," we prevent ourselves
from seeing other ideas as something from which we
could potentially learn.

We can create a new age where all sorts of global ideas
come alive again. Given the personal and societal crises
we face today, these ideas may be our best chance.

How We Have Viewed Asian Ideas

Some reading this book might feel that Asian ideas have
already come alive for the West. Buddhism became enor-
mously popular here several decades ago, bringing with it
all sorts of Buddhist-inspired ideas: meditation, mindfulness, retreats. Many of us in the West have long felt an
emptiness—a sense that our big ideas have let us down.
We have been on a quest for other viable approaches that
will help us live more fulfilling lives.

But there are significant problems with how Buddhism has been appropriated to fit directly into a Western
mind-set and model. Buddhism appealed initially because
it seemed to provide an antidote to our ambition and

greed. Buddhism and the East were romanticized as the polar opposites of the harried, avaricious West. But Buddhism has, for the most part, been misread, further entrenching some of the more dangerous aspects of Western notions of the individual self.

Take mindfulness, for example. It is based on the concept of detaching yourself and looking upon the world and each moment nonjudgmentally, so that things no longer bother you. Mindfulness is hyped widely as a popular technique for gaining peace and serenity in our fast-paced lives. Today it is even promoted as a tool for productivity and effectiveness by business schools, corporations, and the military.

But mindfulness was intended to *break down* the self. Buddhism is the doctrine of *no* self, and Buddhist practices as a whole are designed to do away with the notion that any sort of individual self exists. Yet many of these aspects of Buddhism have been discarded, and instead, it has often been distorted as a way of looking within and embracing the self. It has become a form of exotic self-help: the doctrine of no self utilized to help people feel better about themselves.

More recently, other Asian ideas have also been reinterpreted as coherent ideologies: Daoism, say, or even Confucianism. They have been stripped of their power and recast as somehow being about learning to accept the world as it is and to accept your place within it.

These idealistic readings are the flip side of the Western view of the East as traditional and backward. In this rendition, Asia represents ancient wisdom about a wiser, more integrated, and ideal way to live. But if feeling better means accepting your true self, harmonizing with the world, and being at peace with that, this is a short step from encouraging people to accept their lot in life and play into a traditional worldview that life is predetermined. *We* become complacent and detached, surrendering the opportunity for self-cultivation.

We have folded these notions into a worldview in which the West determines the direction of history and provides the lens through which we see everything. This keeps us from seeing them for what they really are and from recognizing their great potential. As our philosophers have shown us, there are many different viable ways to break down a world in which everything is determined by what we're born with, and move toward one in which humans can flourish.

The opposite of mindlessness and complacency is not mindfulness. It is engagement. The ideas we have traced in this book are immensely pragmatic, rooted in our everyday world and our everyday lives. Each of these texts questioned how best to break from passivity and alter the world in which we live.

The Promise of a Fragmented World

We already know many of the things we have learned about in this book. We already practice aspects of them in our lives. Our Chinese philosophers enable us to name and perceive consciously impulses and behaviors we might otherwise dismiss as irrelevant because they don't fit into our notions of agency and sincerity. They show us that when we think we're being active, we're actually being passive; that when we think we're being true to ourselves, we're boxing in ourselves. They teach us to recognize that the world is unpredictable, and that we grow by living "as if," not by seeking authenticity.

These thinkers all had different views about what makes for a good life. But they are connected by their opposition to the ideas that there is an unchangeable past that binds us, a unified order in the cosmos to which we should adhere, a set of rational laws we should follow, and ethical doctrines handed down that we should heed.

The challenge our philosophers present is this: *Think what your life would be like if you assumed none of those things to be true.*

Our attempts to build a coherent, stable, noncapricious world have taken many forms. For some, it might be a set of universal ethical rules, similar to that of the Mohists. It might be a Kantian code of rational, moral laws we follow, no matter the circumstances. Or perhaps it is a belief in a unified cosmos with which we seek to harmonize. In our most recent rendition, that greater truth is embodied by the authentic self that we must discover within.

We now know that ideas like these existed in one form or another in early China too. But our philosophers viewed the world very differently. They saw us as living in a fragmented and fractured world where people constantly treat one another in all too human ways. They saw us in endless conflict and imperfect relationships.

Westerners tend to look at the Chinese ancestor-worship ritual and take it to mean that the Chinese were always listening to the dead and living in their shadows. Thinkers such as Weber viewed the ritual through the lens of sincerity. His interpretation was that people performing the ritual believed sincerely that the world was as harmonious as the ritual portrayed it to be.

But, in fact, the participants in this ritual knew perfectly well that it didn't reflect reality. They knew they lived in a fragmented world, but that was exactly why they needed the ritual, to allow them to break with messy real life and to play out imaginative possibilities. The ritual helped people not to follow the past but to create a different future. Through as-if ritual, descendants worked with the ghosts that haunted them and created a new version of the past. This was an ongoing process. Those ancestors were never fully put in their place.

But this is why the ritual was repeated again and again. Slowly, over time, there was a progression. By their actions, the living were saying, "This is how we could live our lives if we viewed the past this way." And as they reconstructed the past over and over, they really did begin to live differently.

We can learn something from this too. Our attempts at repairing our own fractured world inevitably are insufficient or even fail. Metaphorically speaking, ghosts—or more literally, our pasts—haunt us to varying degrees. But if we live in a broken world haunted by our pasts—our difficult relationships, our work hardships, our losses, our many inevitable missteps—we need to engage in the equivalent of the ancestor ritual. We must cultivate our emotions with other people repeatedly as we work on constructing a better world. When we can accept how limited we are by the past, by the negative forces within us, and by the fragility of human relationships, our own relationships have limitless potential to be refined and transformed. Caring for one another is hard work. It requires endless awareness, adaptation, and responsiveness. But it is one of the most important and rewarding things that we human beings do.

In this fractured and fragmented world, it's up to us to generate order. We are the ones who construct and give pattern to the world—not by getting rid of the unwieldy human emotions, the messy stuff that is us, but by beginning right there. And we do this through daily self-cultivation: working through our rituals to improve the way we relate to those around us; cultivating energies in our bodies so that we can live with more vitality; training our hearts and minds to work through daily decisions in a powerfully different way; and resisting our tendency to cut ourselves off from experience, so that we become constantly receptive to new things.

The process of building a better world never ends because our attempts to build better relationships are never finished. But as we learn how to better our relationships, we will learn how to alter situations and thereby create infinite numbers of new worlds. We will open ourselves up to the possibilities in these philosophical ideas that point the way to a good life.

If the world is fragmented, then it gives us every opportunity to construct things anew. It begins with the smallest things in our daily lives, from which we change everything. If we begin there, then everything is up to us.

Acknowledgments

First and foremost, we would like to thank the thousands of students that Michael has been privileged to teach over the years. Their intellectual curiosity and passion for ideas have been a constant source of inspiration to him.

We are grateful to our agent, Gillian MacKenzie, for seeing the great potential in a book on Chinese philosophy; publisher Jonathan Karp, for so warmly backing this project; our editor, Priscilla Painton, for keen edits and unflagging enthusiasm; Sophia Jimenez, for ever-reliable support and assistance; Phil Metcalf, for superb copyedits; and the fantastic Simon & Schuster publicity and marketing team: Cary Goldstein, Richard Rohrer, and Dana Trocker. We are ever grateful to the splendid Allison Devereux and Kirsten Wolf for their help. Heartfelt thanks go to Camilla Ferrier, Jessica Woollard, Jemma McDonagh, and Georgina Le Grice at the Marsh Agency, as well as all the editors who are enthusiastically publishing the book abroad.

In addition, we are especially appreciative to Daniel Crewe of Viking UK, who took the time to offer invaluable editorial comments and suggestions. Grateful thanks also go to Samuel Douglas, Jennifer Margulis, and Laura Simeon, who commented so astutely on earlier drafts of this book, as well to Jen Guidera, Roland Lamb, Elizabeth Malkin, Adam Mitchell, Katherine Ozment, and Jeannie Suk for their support.

Deepest thanks go to our families, without whose patience and support this book could not have been written.

Finally, with great gratitude, we thank each other. This was a true collaboration: the discussions of the philosophers were developed in Michael's class, while Christine added in modern-day examples and wrote about the ideas of these thinkers for a contemporary audience. The result is a book that greatly exceeds what either of us could have done on our own.

Resources and Further Reading

To read relevant passages from the original works
of Chinese philosophy, see our free e-book
Confucius, Mencius, Laozi, Zhuangzi, Xunzi: Selected Passages,
available on Kindle, Nook, and the iBook Store.

A note: many of the texts discussed in *The Path* are thought to have been created over lengthy periods of time and compiled in different ways by different editors. However, throughout history, they have been read and discussed as coherent texts representing the ideas of the sole philosopher in question, and for readability's sake, we continue in that tradition by using the names of the major philosophers; for example, rather than writing "The text of the *Mencius* argues," we write "Mencius argues."

An excellent anthology of most of the philosophers we discussed can be found in Philip J. Ivanhoe and Bryan W. Van Norden, eds., *Readings in Classical Chinese Philosophy* (Indianapolis: Hackett, 2005).

For full translations, we suggest:

Burton Watson, trans., *The Complete Works of Zhuangzi (Translations from the Asian Classics)* (New York: Columbia University Press, 2013).

D. C. Lau, trans., *The Analects* (New York: Penguin Books, 1979).

Mencius (New York: Penguin Books, 2005).

Tao Te Ching [by Lao Tzu] (New York: Penguin Books, 1985).

Harold D. Roth, *Original Tao: Inward Training (Nei-yeh) and the Foundations of Taoist Mysticism (Translations from the Asian Classics)* (New York: Columbia University Press, 2004).

The Age of Philosophy

For further reading:

Jared Diamond, *Guns, Germs, and Steel: The Fates of Human Societies* (New York: W. W. Norton, 2005).

Ian Morris, *Why the West Rules—for Now: The Patterns of History, and What They Reveal About the Future* (New York: Farrar, Straus and Giroux, 2010).

Confucius

On "as if" from a larger philosophical perspective, see:

Hans Vaihinger, *The Philosophy of 'As if': A System of the Theoretical, Practical and Religious Fictions of Mankind,* translated by C. K. Ogden, 2nd ed. (New York: Harcourt, Brace and Company, 1935).

Adam B. Seligman, Robert P. Weller, Michael J. Puett, and Bennett Simon, *Ritual and Its Consequences: An Essay on the Limits of Sincerity* (New York: Oxford University Press, 2008).

On history of please and thank you:

David Graeber, *Debt: The First 5,000 Years* (Brooklyn, NY: Melville House, 2011).

Laozi

On Lincoln:

Garry Wills, *Lincoln at Gettysburg: The Words That Remade America* (New York: Simon & Schuster, 1992).

On the presidential salute:

> Garry Wills, *Bomb Power: The Modern Presidency and the National Security State* (New York: Penguin Books, 2010).

Inward Training

On self-divinization:

> Michael J. Puett, *To Become a God: Cosmology, Sacrifice, and Self-Divinization in Early China* (Cambridge, MA: Harvard University Asia Center, 2002).

Zhuangzi

On flow:

> Mihaly Csikszentmihalyi, *Flow: The Psychology of Optimal Experience* (New York: Harper & Row, 1990).

Xunzi

On hand washing:

> Sherwin B. Nuland, *The Doctors' Plague: Germs, Childbed Fever, and the Strange Story of Ignác Semmelweis* (New York: W. W. Norton, 2003).